# Brain Hacks

Life-Changing Strategies to Improve Executive Functioning

## Jett Thompson

Journey Together Ltd

Copyright © 2025 by Journey Together LTD

All rights reserved.

No portion of this book may be reproduced in any form without written permission from the publisher or author, except as permitted by U.S. copyright law.

# Contents

Welcome to the Brain Gym     1

1. Focus Mode     4
2. Executive Function     10
3. Procrastination Fixes     16
4. Brain Fog Be Gone     22
5. Memory Boosters     28
6. Emotional Regulation     34
7. Mindfulness Without the Woo     40
8. Cognitive Flexibility     46
9. Brain-Friendly Routines     52
10. Creativity Hacks     60
11. Learning on Speed     67
12. Neuroplasticity Playground     72
13. Feelings Are Data     78

You Don't Need a New Brain     83

# Welcome to the Brain Gym

## (No Sweat Required)

Let's be real: your brain is doing *a lot*. It's filtering emails, remembering passwords, making decisions, second-guessing those decisions, wondering if that text was too weird, keeping you breathing, and also—surprise—trying to keep you alive.

No wonder you're tired.

In a world that moves fast and expects faster, your brain has become the ultimate multitool. But here's the plot twist nobody tells you: your brain isn't always working *with* you. Sometimes it hoards anxiety. Sometimes it forgets your PIN while you're in line at the ATM. Sometimes it decides that watching 22 dog videos is more important than starting the actual task. (Relatable? Good. You're in the right place.)

**Why Brain Hacks Matter Now More Than Ever**

Because modern life is basically a game of mental whack-a-mole.

We're making more decisions in a day than previous generations made in a week. We're expected to focus through pings, meetings, grocery lists, self-improvement podcasts, and the mental math of "do I *really* need 8 hours of sleep or can I wing it on 5?"

That kind of cognitive load? It adds up. That's where brain hacks come in. Not as "do more" tools, but as "do smarter" ones.

Brain hacks are shortcuts, rewires, and small upgrades that help you work *with* your brain's weird wiring instead of against it. They're how you sidestep burnout, boost your focus, and function like a person who *didn't* leave their keys in the fridge (again).

## You Don't Need a PhD to Outsmart Your Own Brain

Let's bust a myth while we're here: You don't need a neuroscience degree, twelve meditation apps, or a bulletproof morning routine to have a better-functioning brain.

You just need to understand a few key truths about how your brain *really* works—on a Tuesday, in real life, when the caffeine hasn't kicked in yet.

This book skips the jargon and cuts straight to the useful stuff—no ivory tower advice. No guilt. Just practical tricks you can actually use today—even if your mental energy is somewhere between "meh" and "whoops."

## Meet the Brain's Backstage Crew

Every decision you make, every scroll, every snack, every "sure I'll do that even though I'm overloaded" moment—those are influenced by a set of chemical puppeteers behind the curtain:

- **Dopamine**: The thrill-seeker. Loves quick wins and novelty.
- **Serotonin**: The mood stabilizer. Loves sunshine, routine, and not feeling like life is spiraling.
- **Cortisol**: The overachieving alarm bell. Great in a crisis. Bad on loop.
- **Oxytocin**: The warm fuzzy. Loves connection, hugs, and shared snacks.

This book doesn't just talk about them—it shows you how to *work with* them. Because if you learn to speak their language, they'll help you get more done, stay calm under pressure, and maybe even sleep through the night.

**How to Use This Book (Flip, Skim, Dive, or Emergency Browse)**

Think of this book like your brain's instruction manual—written in a way your brain will actually read.

Each chapter tackles a big brain struggle (focus, memory, habits, emotional regulation, etc.) and offers:

- Quick hacks you can test immediately
- Real-life tips that feel like a friend's advice, not a lecture
- No-pressure ways to level up when you're ready

You can read front-to-back like a brain bootcamp, or skip straight to the chapter that screams "YES. That. Help." Lost your focus again? Flip to Focus Hacks. Feeling like a memory-impaired goldfish? Hit the Memory Boosters.

Whatever page you land on, there's something here to help you function just a little better—with less friction, more clarity, and a brain that finally feels like it's on your side.

**Ready to think smarter, not harder?** Welcome to the Shortcut Society for your brain. Let's get hacking.

# Focus Mode

## Find Your Mental Mojo

Focus isn't dead. It's just buried under 37 tabs, 8 notifications, and the deep emotional weight of a group chat that won't stop buzzing. We don't lack attention—we're just surrounded by way too many things screaming "HEY! LOOK AT ME!" at the same time.

This chapter is about silencing the noise (both real and mental) so you can finally get stuff done. Whether your brain is wandering off like a toddler in a toy store or you're just trying to read an email without checking Instagram five times, these hacks will help you lock in without burning out.

Just to clarify—we're not asking you to become a monk, delete your social media, or throw your phone in a lake. This is about low-effort, real-life shifts that help your brain tune out the chaos and reclaim just enough focus to get things done (without feeling like a robot).

### The "Laser Brain" Warm-Up

You know those mornings when your brain feels like it's still buffering? You've technically been awake for an hour, but mentally you're just... hovering. Opening a tab. Staring at it. Closing it again. Rummaging in the fridge like clarity might be hiding behind the hummus.

Starting your day cold like this is a recipe for drift, distraction, and checking your email four times without reading anything.

Would you run a marathon without warming up? (Trick question: you wouldn't run a marathon at all.) But the same logic applies. Your brain needs time to shift gears—from "scroll mode" to "focus mode." The first few minutes of your workday shouldn't be a test—they should be a warm-up. And if you set it up right, your brain will follow your lead.

- **Hack 1: The Five-Minute Mental Wind-Up**

Pick one small thing—like tidying your desk, writing one sentence, or opening the file you've been avoiding. That little start creates momentum. The trick isn't diving in—it's just *showing up*. Focus often arrives *after* you begin.

- **Hack 2: Set the Scene**

Lighting, sound, and clutter all affect brain energy. Tidy space = less background mental clutter. Bonus points if you light a candle or play lo-fi beats. Make your brain feel like it just walked into a spa for productivity.

- **Hack 3: Decision-Free Mornings**

Set yourself up the night before—clothes, to-do list, coffee prep. When your brain doesn't have to make a hundred little choices first thing, it's way more likely to slip into focus mode. Less friction, more flow. Future you says thanks.

## Pomodoro 2.0 – Focus Sprints That Actually Stick

The original Pomodoro Technique (25 minutes on, 5 off) is great... unless you're someone who finds 25 minutes too short to get into the zone or too long to even *start*. The point isn't to follow a strict timer. It's to help your brain alternate between deep work and recovery—without falling into distraction limbo.

- **Hack 4: Try Custom Sprints**

Experiment with what actually works for you. Some people love 25/5. Others need 45/15. The key is setting a *clear* work chunk and *protecting* that time like it's sacred. Focus is personal. There's no "perfect ratio," just the one that gets you moving.

- **Hack 5: Make the Break Count**

Don't just doom-scroll during your 5 minutes. Move. Stretch. Breathe. Stare out a window like you're in a dramatic movie. Your brain resets better when the break is offline.

- **Hack 6: The Alarm Clock Trick**

Use a physical timer. Not your phone. If your focus tool *is also* your distraction device, we have a problem. Use a kitchen timer. Or an old-school alarm. Anything that doesn't also offer memes.

- **Hack 7: End with a Cliffhanger**

Stop working mid-sentence or mid-idea. Seriously. Your brain will want to return to it later, which makes getting started next time 10x easier.

## The Background Noise Equation

Not everyone thrives in silence. For some brains, quiet is too loud—you start hearing the fridge hum, overanalyzing that one sentence in your email, or falling down the rabbit hole of your own thoughts. Your focus drifts into weird memories or the sound of your own thoughts.

That's why background sound is a legit focus tool. It creates a mental buffer—a layer of soothing noise that lets your concentration settle.

- **Hack 8: Find Your Focus Soundtrack**

**Lo-fi beats:** great for writing or solo tasks

**Brown noise:** blocks external sounds without melody distractions

**Nature sounds:** for chill-but-alert vibes

**Instrumentals only:** lyrics are for karaoke, not deep focus

What works for one person's flow state might be someone else's nap soundtrack—so test and trust your ears.

- **Hack 9: Audio Anchoring**

Always use the same playlist for deep work. Over time, your brain will associate that sound with focus, like a Pavlovian productivity bell.

- **Hack 10: Soundproof Your Environment**

Can't control the chaos? Use noise-canceling headphones—even without music. Muting the world is sometimes all your brain needs.

- **Hack 11: The Noise Audit**

Don't force brown noise if it grates on your nerves. Some folks thrive on white noise. Others need light coffee-shop chatter. Your brain, your rules—pay attention to what actually helps.

## App-Blockers, Dopamine Detoxes, and the "Do Not Disturb" Gospel

Let's talk about dopamine. It's your brain's favorite chemical. It rewards you for novelty, stimulation, and quick wins. Your phone? It's a dopamine factory. Every notification, message, or shiny red bubble is a treat dispenser.

And you're the squirrel.

The goal here isn't to give up dopamine—it's to *redirect it* toward the tasks you care about.

- **Hack 12: App-Blocker That Means It**

Try FocusMe, Freedom, or Forest. Block your biggest distraction apps for a set time. Your future self will say thank you. Possibly with tears.

- **Hack 13: Do Not Disturb = Default Mode**

Set "Do Not Disturb" on your phone and computer as your *default*, not an exception. Let real humans call twice in an emergency. The rest can wait.

- **Hack 14: Detox Days**

Once a week, log off for an hour (or more) on purpose. Your brain needs time without stimulation. You'll come back sharper—and maybe even less grumpy.

- **Hack 15: The Dopamine Delay Rule**

Craving social media or a snack? Do *one* productive thing first. Earn the hit. Turn temptation into motivation.

- **Hack 16: Make It Inconvenient**

Sign out of your most distracting apps. Put them on the third screen of your phone. Add friction. Your brain is lazy—use that to your advantage.

## The Magic of Monotasking

Your brain can't multitask. Full stop. It can only switch between tasks—rapidly and sloppily—while pretending to be productive. Every switch burns a little fuel. Every context shift costs time, accuracy, and energy.

Monotasking is the cheat code you forgot existed.

- **Hack 17: The Task Stack Rule**

Write down your top 3 tasks. Do them *one at a time.* Highlight or strike through when done. Visual progress is both satisfying and effective.

- **Hack 18: The Phone in Jail Trick**

Put your phone in another room. Or a drawer. Or an actual lockbox if needed. If it's not within arm's reach, it's not within mental reach either.

- **Hack 19: The 20-Minute Test**

Give one task your *undivided* attention for 20 minutes. If it still sucks after that, you can switch. But 9 times out of 10, you'll be too deep in the zone to care.

- **Hack 20: Block the Tabs**

Only keep 1–3 tabs open. Use extensions like OneTab or Tab Wrangler. A crowded browser = a scattered brain.


## TL;DR Recap – Focus Without the Fight

- **Start small** to build momentum
- **Use sprints** with real breaks (not just new distractions)
- **Control the noise**—find your focus soundtrack
- **Set boundaries** with tech—your phone is not the boss
- **Monotask** like your brain depends on it (because it does)

**Focus Isn't a Superpower—It's a Strategy**

You're not lazy. You're overloaded. And most of what's stealing your focus isn't your fault—it's your environment, your tech, and your wiring.

But you can fight back. With small shifts, new habits, and a few well-timed hacks, you *can* train your brain to stop chasing shiny things and start chasing results.

Focus isn't about being perfect. It's about creating a space where your brain can finally breathe—and do its best work without a 37-tab circus.

Now close the extras, put your phone somewhere inconvenient, and let yourself lock in—even if it's just for 15 good minutes. That's where the magic starts.

# Executive Function
## Make the Smart Part Work

Executive function is basically your brain's CEO—except it doesn't wear a suit, and it's constantly undercaffeinated. It's the system behind planning your week, switching tasks, remembering deadlines, resisting impulse Amazon buys, and not screaming when your inbox hits 99+.

When this system is humming, life flows. When it's overloaded, everything feels like a mess—even if nothing's technically wrong.

This chapter is about giving your brain's management team the hacks they need to keep things smooth, focused, and a little less chaotic. Let's upgrade the way your brain organizes, decides, and executes—without the corporate buzzwords.

**What Even Is Executive Function? (A Real-Life Cheat Sheet)**

If you've ever walked into a room and forgotten why, that's not a brain fail—it's a momentary executive function glitch. These mental skills handle your time, attention, memory, and emotional control. Basically, they're the behind-the-scenes crew making life doable.

But here's the kicker: they're not fixed. You can train and improve them—without a brain boot camp. You just need the right tools.

- **Hack 21: Executive Inventory**

List your daily "fail points." Are you late? Forgetful? Scattered? That's your brain showing you which executive functions need backup. Awareness is step one.

- **Hack 22: The "Brain as Manager" Trick**

Visualize your brain running a team. Attention is the intern, impulse control is security, and memory is the project manager. If one's slacking, support it like you would a teammate.

- **Hack 23: Build in Buffers**

Don't pack your schedule back-to-back. Executive function needs breathing room to switch gears. Add 5–10 minute buffers between tasks to reset mentally.

- **Hack 24: Mental Checkpoints**

Set two or three "check-in" moments during your day—like after lunch or before switching tasks. Pause, breathe, and ask: *What was I doing? What's next?* These mini status updates help your brain recalibrate, rather than spiraling into distraction.

## Memory Shortcuts That Stick (and Don't Rely on Sticky Notes)

Your brain forgets things. If your to-dos vanish into the mental abyss five minutes after you think of them. That's not a bug—it's a feature. It's trying to prioritize what matters (and apparently, that's song lyrics from 2004). The trick isn't forcing yourself to remember more. It's giving your brain smarter ways to store and retrieve what you actually need.

These hacks are about memory boosters that fit into your daily life—nothing complicated, just stuff that sticks. No flashcards required.

- **Hack 25: Use the Rule of Three**

Our brains love threes. Limit your daily to-do list to three priorities max. This isn't underachieving—it's realistic cognitive bandwidth.

- **Hack 26: The "Memory Trigger" Method**

Attach new info to something already locked in. Example: need to remember to send a report after lunch? Leave your coffee mug on your keyboard. It's weird. It works.

- **Hack 27: Chunking 101**

Break info into chunks. Instead of 247193, think 24–71–93. Works for numbers, ideas, even people's names. Your brain processes patterns, not floods.

- **Hack 28: Speak It to Keep It**

Saying something out loud reinforces it. Repeating a name or a plan—even if you sound like a weirdo in the hallway—locks it in deeper.

- **Hack 29: The Memory Lane Review**

Do a mental recap at the end of your day. Walk through what you did, who you spoke to, and anything unfinished. Reflection builds memory muscle.

## Planning Without Panic: Chunking, Blocking, Batching

Planning doesn't need to be color-coded chaos. You don't need a fancy app or a life coach—just a system that helps you see what's ahead and not lose your mind in the process. It means choosing *how* and *when* you use your brain's energy wisely.

Great plans reduce friction, overwhelm, and "where do I even start?" paralysis. These methods work with your brain, not against it. Because once you learn to batch, block, and chunk your time like a pro, you'll stop feeling like your to-do list is yelling at you.

- **Hack 30: Time Blocking for Mortals**

Split your day into blocks: deep work, admin tasks, meetings, breaks. Doesn't need to be perfect. Just needs to help you see where your energy should go.

- **Hack 31: Task Batching Like a Pro**

Do similar tasks together—emails, errands, reports. Switching contexts constantly drains you more than you realize. Batch it and be done.

- **Hack 32: Reverse Planning**

Start with the outcome and work backward. Want a report done by Friday? Block time on Wednesday and Thursday to work on it. Reverse planning prevents last-minute scrambles.

- **Hack 33: Make It Visual**

Sticky notes on a wall, a kanban board, a whiteboard of doom—your brain loves seeing stuff laid out. It brings clarity and a weird sense of peace.

- **Hack 34: 15-Minute Planning Sesh**

Take 15 minutes on Sunday or Monday morning to sketch your week. No detail overload—just major goals and priorities. A tiny habit with a big payoff.

## "Decision Fatigue" Is Real – And It's Eating Your Brain

Every choice you make chips away at your mental energy. Pick an outfit, reply to a message, choose a cereal—it all adds up. By midday, your decision tank is empty, your brain's done making good decisions, and wants a nap or a doughnut.

This section is about saving your brain from burnout by reducing tiny, sneaky choices that drain your focus. Fewer decisions = more brainpower for the things that actually matter.

- **Hack 35: Automate the Basics**

The same breakfast, the same shirt color, and the same playlist. The more decisions you remove from your mornings, the more brainpower you preserve for actual work.

- **Hack 36: Create Default Options**

What's your go-to lunch spot? Backup project plan? Plan B when it rains? Pre-decided defaults stop you from spiraling every time something shifts.

- **Hack 37: Schedule High-Energy Tasks Early**

Don't save the hard stuff for 4 p.m. Your brain is sharpest earlier in the day (yes, even if you're a "night owl"). Use peak hours for key decisions.

- **Hack 38: Say No Faster**

Indecision burns energy. Set a 60-second rule: if it's not a "heck yes" or clearly valuable, say no and move on.

- **Hack 39: Decision-Free Zones**

Designate parts of your day where you make zero decisions. Lunch hour = recharge only. Late night = no work chats. Your brain will thank you.

## Routines That Save Your Sanity (and Bandwidth)

Routines aren't boring—they're brain fuel. When your day follows a familiar rhythm, your mind doesn't have to scramble for what comes next. That frees up energy for real thinking, not just surviving.

Good routines are like mental scaffolding: they hold up your day so you don't collapse. They should be flexible, low-effort, and built around your life. You don't need a 5 a.m. bootcamp vibe. You just need some smart patterns that take the pressure off.

- **Hack 40: The Anchor Routine**

Pick one consistent habit to center your day around—morning coffee + plan review, lunchtime walk, or end-of-day brain dump. Anchors create structure.

- **Hack 41: Bookend Your Days**

Morning and evening routines matter more than the messy middle. Start and end your day with intention, even if the middle is controlled chaos.

- **Hack 42: Habit Stacking**

Pair a new habit with an existing one. Want to stretch more? Do it while brushing your teeth. Want to review tasks? Pair it with coffee time. The brain loves routine piggybacks.

- **Hack 43: Use Triggers, Not Willpower**

Set alarms, visual cues, or leave notes in strategic places. Make your environment remind you, not your memory.

- **Hack 44: Routine Reset Days**

Once a month, audit your routines. What's helping? What's draining you? Tweak one small thing to keep your rhythm aligned with real life.

**Let's Wrap it Up**

Executive function isn't about being perfect—it's about working smarter with what your brain's already doing. When you build systems that reduce friction, free up memory, and simplify choices, you stop wasting mental energy on the *how* and start getting traction on the *what*.

Small upgrades in how you think, plan, and decide = major impact.

You don't need to be a master organizer. You just need a few hacks that help your brain do what it already wants to do: solve, sort, and get things done.

# Procrastination Fixes
## The Art of the Start

You know that weird limbo when you're staring at your to-do list like it's written in a foreign language? Where opening one email feels like climbing Everest, and somehow reorganizing your spice rack becomes wildly urgent? That's procrastination. And no, it doesn't mean you're broken, lazy, or doomed to live in deadline chaos forever.

Procrastination isn't about time—it's about emotion. Your brain is trying to protect you from discomfort: fear of failing, fear of starting, or fear of just being bored. So it throws up distractions, perfectionism, or tells you that "now isn't the right time." (Spoiler: It never is.)

This chapter is your field guide to hacking that avoidance loop. We're not fighting procrastination with guilt or discipline—we're sneaking around it. It's not about force. It's about friction. Lower it, and suddenly, starting becomes simple. Let's learn how to make motion easier than inertia.

### Why You Wait (and What Your Brain Thinks It's Doing)

Procrastination isn't always a sign of laziness. Often, it's your brain trying to avoid discomfort—like confusion, fear of failure, or just good ol' boredom. It's risk management, emotional regulation, and mental energy conservation all rolled into one. "I'll do it tomorrow."

But here's the catch: waiting rarely makes things easier. The emotional weight grows. The task looms. And now you're stressed *and* behind. The trick is learning why you delay—and then making the start feel easier than the stall.

- **Hack 45: Name the Resistance**

Ask yourself: What exactly am I avoiding? Is it boredom? Fear? Uncertainty? Naming the discomfort makes it easier to shrink. You're not avoiding *the task*—you're avoiding a feeling.

- **Hack 46: The Starting Ritual**

Create a consistent "start cue"—tea, timer, same playlist, same hoodie. This tells your brain, "We're shifting gears now." Rituals beat willpower every time.

- **Hack 47: Do the Fun Part First**

If there's one small part of the task you *don't* dread, start there. Hook your brain with the easiest win.

- **Hack 48: Turn "Later" into a Time Slot**

When your brain says "not now," pin it down. Decide *exactly when*. Put it on your calendar—even if it's just 20 minutes tomorrow. Giving procrastination a time and place tricks your brain into thinking the task is under control, reducing anxiety and the need to avoid it entirely.

- **Hack 49: Visualize the Consequence**

Instead of imagining the task, picture what happens if you *don't* do it. Missed deadlines, last-minute panic, awkward follow-ups. Sometimes a gentle scare tactic works better than a pep talk.

## The "2-Minute Momentum" Hack

If something takes less than 2 minutes, just do it now. That's the classic rule. But there's more: the 2-minute trick isn't just about knocking off tiny tasks—it's about unlocking momentum. Most things feel bigger and scarier before you begin, but the second you start, your brain often realizes, "Oh... this isn't that bad."

Starting isn't a commitment to finish—it's just breaking the seal. And once that seal's broken, your brain usually shrugs and keeps going. It's like mental inertia in reverse: a tiny nudge forward makes the next step easier, then the next one, and suddenly you're rolling.

- **Hack 50: The "Start Timer" Game**

Set a timer for 2 minutes. You only have to work until it rings. 90% of the time, you'll keep going. The hardest part was starting.

- **Hack 51: Open the Tab, Don't Do the Thing**

Just open the document. Just put on your shoes. You don't have to run, write, or reply—yet. But guess what? Now you're one tiny step in, and that counts.

- **Hack 52: Create a Launch List**

Make a list of 5 "micro-starts"—actions that take less than 2 minutes. When you're stuck, pick one. Momentum is built, not wished into existence.

- **Hack 53: Micro Commitments Jar**

Write down 10 tiny actions (e.g., open doc, highlight text, type one line) on scraps of paper. Keep them in a jar or box. When you're stuck, pull one at random. It turns into a game—and instantly lowers the pressure.

## Anti-Overwhelm Trick: Shrink the Task, Not the Goal

Big goals are intimidating. That's why your brain responds with the mental equivalent of hiding under a blanket. "Write a report" sounds like a mountain. "Write a sentence" sounds doable. The overwhelm isn't from the work—it's from not knowing where to begin.

That's the trick: don't downsize your ambition, just reduce the starting load. Break the big, blurry goal into small, concrete steps your brain can actually process. Think LEGO bricks, not skyscrapers. The goal stays the same—only the entry point changes.

- **Hack 54: Name the Next Action**

Not "plan the project"—just "write the first bullet point." Get absurdly specific. Vague = delay. Specific = action.

- **Hack 55: The Ten-Minute Slice**

Commit to working on one slice of the task for 10 minutes only. If you keep going—great. If not, you still won.

- **Hack 56: The "What's Stopping Me?" Scan**

Write down every reason you're stuck. Then, problem-solve each one like a puzzle. You don't need motivation—you need clarity.

- **Hack 57: Task Matryoshka**

Like nesting dolls, each major task has smaller ones within it. Keep breaking it down until it's laughably doable. Then start with the tiniest one.

- **Hack 58: Label the Level of Effort**

Add a quick tag to your task list: [Easy], [Medium], [Brain-Heavy]. When overwhelmed, just knock out the [Easy] ones first. Progress creates confidence, which fuels bigger effort.

## Future You Is Lazy – Use That

Present You is always overcommitting. Future You? A mythological creature who somehow has more energy, motivation, and time than Present You ever does. That's the person you're always assigning tasks to—"I'll do it tomorrow," "Monday Me will sort it out," "Future Me can totally handle this." Spoiler: Future You is just You, but more tired.

Instead of pretending you'll magically have more energy tomorrow, start designing your day *as if* you'll be tired, distracted, and lazy—because that's usually the truth.

- **Hack 59: Build "Lazy-Proof" Plans**

Set up your workspace the night before. Leave your to-do list open. If a task needs a document, have it ready. Make things so easy, Future You just has to click.

- **Hack 60: Time-Lock the Temptations**

Put your distractions in digital jail. Schedule app blockers during work hours. Out of sight = less friction.

- **Hack 61: Use Pre-Commitment**

Tell someone you're doing the thing. Set a fake deadline. Make it social, scheduled, or visible—because guilt is a surprisingly effective motivator.

- **Hack 62: Default to Done**

Leave tabs, files, or half-started tasks open so you're forced to return. Your brain hates unfinished business.

- **Hack 63: Plant Friction for Bad Habits**

Make procrastination harder. Delete quick-access tabs. Log out of distractions. Move your charger to another room. If Lazy You have to *work* to avoid work, they might not bother.

## Rewards, Reminders, and Ridiculous Bribes (They Work)

Your brain doesn't run on duty—it runs on dopamine. That's why even the idea of a treat can push you through the "meh" of getting started. So yes, you're allowed to bribe yourself. You're not cheating. You're negotiating.

Small rewards and strategic nudges turn procrastination into progress—especially when they're just fun enough to make work worth starting.

- **Hack 64: Bribe Like You Mean It**

"Finish this task, and I'll get a cookie." Or an episode. Or 5 minutes of guilt-free scrolling. Pick something your brain *wants now*, not something noble and distant.

- **Hack 65: Visual Progress = Instant Reward**

Use a checklist, a tracker, and a post-it wall. Seeing progress *is* a reward. Bonus: it motivates Future You too.

- **Hack 66: Create a "Done" Jar**

Each time you complete a task, write it down and toss it in. At the end of the week, read them back and marvel at your awesomeness. It's silly. It works.

- **Hack 67: Alarm Nudges**

Set fun or weird reminders that pop up with encouraging messages like "You're 20 minutes from glory!" or "Start now, complain later."

- **Hack 68: The Ridiculous Bet**

Make an absurd deal with yourself: "If I finish this by 3 p.m., I get to wear pajamas to my next Zoom call" or "I can watch one cat video for every 20 minutes of writing." The sillier, the better—it adds novelty and motivation.

## Brain Hack Debrief

Procrastination isn't a character flaw—it's a clever brain strategy that just backfires. Your mind isn't trying to sabotage you. It's trying to protect you from discomfort, decision fatigue, or the terrifying blank stare of a new project. The key is to stop shaming it and start outsmarting it.

By lowering friction, creating momentum, and rewarding even the tiniest steps, you're rewiring how your brain responds to action. You're building a launch pad instead of trying to climb a wall.

So next time you're stuck, don't wait for some magical surge of motivation to strike. Use a 2-minute trick. Shrink the task. Bribe yourself. Trick your brain with fun, with structure, or with the knowledge that Future You is just a slippery little gremlin. Start ugly. Start small. But most importantly—start.

# Brain Fog Be Gone

## Mental Clarity Tricks

We've all had that moment: staring at the screen, blinking, wondering what day it is, what task we were just doing, and whether we've drunk any water since 1996.

Welcome to brain fog. It's not dramatic like burnout. It's sneakier—like mental quicksand. You're technically awake, technically working, but nothing's quite *clicking*. Thoughts feel fuzzy, decisions feel harder than they should, and even typing a simple email feels like it's being routed through five different continents before it reaches your fingers.

The problem? Brain fog isn't a one-time glitch. It's what happens when your brain—your beautifully complex command center—is running low on fuel, clarity, or space. But the good news is this: mental clarity is something you can reboot faster than you think.

This chapter isn't about drinking turmeric tea in the forest (though go for it if that's your thing). These are real, fast, practical clarity tricks—designed for the tired, distracted, and digitally-overloaded brain you have right now.

Let's switch the fog lights on.

### Sleep, Hydration, Movement – The Boring Brilliance Trio

You know this already—but we're going to say it again louder for the brains in the back: your mental clarity *starts* with your physical foundation.

Your body is your brain's power source, and when you ignore it, the consequences show up as mental sluggishness, forgetfulness, and a general "ugh" feeling that follows you around like a foggy cloud.

- **Hack 69: Hydrate Like You Mean It**

Mild dehydration (just 1–2% loss) can tank your focus, memory, and mood. So here's a no-excuse rule: drink a full glass of water *before* your coffee. Not after. Before. Your brain is 75% water—don't let it run on empty.

- **Hack 70: The 90-Minute Movement Rule**

Set a timer. Every 90 minutes, you move. Stand, stretch, shake it out, walk around the room like a confused detective—whatever works. Just interrupt the fog. Bodies in motion, clear heads in motion.

- **Hack 71: Lights Out = Brain On**

Protect your sleep like it's your job. One solid night can sharpen your thinking more than any productivity app. Try a tech cut-off 30 minutes before bed and a warm shower to wind down. It's not fancy—it's effective.

- **Hack 72: Eat the Rainbow, Not the Rollercoaster**

Avoid the sugar spike/sugar crash loop. Pack your meals and snacks with protein, complex carbs, and color. Brain fuel isn't just about eating—it's about eating smart.

## The Reset Ritual (5-Minute Mental Cleanout)

When your brain is scrambled eggs, it doesn't need a full-on life overhaul. It just needs a reset button. That's where the 5-minute mental cleanout comes in.

Think of this like a system reboot. A way to declutter your brain, sort your thoughts, and regain a sense of control—without needing a week-long retreat or deleting society.

- **Hack 73: Do a "Mind Dump" on Paper**

Set a timer for 2–3 minutes. Write *everything* that's in your head—tasks, worries, random thoughts. No structure. No censoring. When it's all out, you'll instantly feel clearer. Your brain was never meant to hold the to-do list.

- **Hack 74: Sort the Chaos with Three Circles**

Draw three circles on a page:

1. **Do now**

2. **Do later**

3. **Doesn't actually matter**

Move your mind-dump items into each. You just turned noise into action—and action into calm.

- **Hack 75: The 5-Things Grounding Game**

Name 5 things you can see, 4 you can touch, 3 you can hear, 2 you can smell, 1 you can taste. It's simple, but it pulls you out of panic and back into the present. Works especially well before big meetings or after digital overload.

- **Hack 76: One Deep Breath, One Clear Intention**

Before switching tasks, stop and breathe deeply—just once. Then ask: "What's the *next best* thing I can do right now?" That clarity is gold. You don't need a perfect plan. You need one right step.

## Digital Drain: How to Clear Your Tabs (and Your Mind)

If your computer has 30 tabs open and your brain feels the same way, that's not a coincidence. Your mental RAM can only hold so much.

Digital clutter isn't just annoying—it's mentally exhausting. Clearing the screen chaos is one of the fastest ways to feel mentally lighter.

Let's declutter the chaos machine.

- **Hack 77: The Tab Triage**

Go through your open browser tabs and ask:

- Is this task finished? Close.

- Is this a reference for later? Bookmark.

- Is this guilt in a tab? Delete.

You don't need "aspirational tabs" haunting your week. Keep what serves you now.

- **Hack 78: "One App at a Time" Mode**

Close everything except the one app or window you're using. That's it. The others are banished. You'll be amazed at how quiet your brain feels when it's not surrounded by digital noise.

- **Hack 79: Clear the Notification Jungle**

Go through your phone and desktop. Turn off *non-essential* notifications (yes, even the breaking news ones). You don't need 53 reminders that the world is on fire. Protect your mental real estate.

- **Hack 80: Screen-Free Start**

Try 10 minutes in the morning before checking your phone. No scrolling. No emails. Just stretch, breathe, make tea, exist. Let *you* set the tone—not the notifications.

## The Gut-Brain Connection (Why Your Lunch Affects Your Focus)

Your gut isn't just about digestion—it's like a second brain that influences mood, energy, and mental clarity. Yes, what's on your plate can either sharpen your thinking or send you straight into brain sludge.

Science is starting to catch up with what our bodies already know: your gut health has a massive impact on your mental clarity. It's not just about digestion—it's about cognition.

If you've ever felt mentally cloudy after lunch, this is your body trying to tell you something. Let's listen.

- **Hack 81: Eat for Your Microbiome**

Incorporate fermented foods (yogurt, kimchi, sauerkraut) and prebiotic fiber (bananas, oats, apples). Your gut bacteria thrive on variety—and they're in charge of some pretty big mood and focus hormones.

- **Hack 82: The Protein Power Lunch**

A lunch full of simple carbs = nap city. A lunch with lean protein, veggies, and healthy fat = steady focus. Eggs, chicken, lentils, tuna, tofu—pick your favorite brain-fuel combo.

- **Hack 83: Track the Brain Fog Foods**

For 3 days, jot down what you eat and how you feel 1 hour later. You might start noticing patterns—maybe dairy slows you down, or maybe coffee sharpens you until it backfires. Personal clarity starts with personal data.

- **Hack 84: Don't Skip the Damn Meal**

Skipping lunch isn't noble—it's self-sabotage. When you skip fuel, your brain scrapes the bottom of the barrel. Eat the lunch. Drink the water. You're not a machine, and that's a good thing.

## The Power of Pausing (a.k.a. Strategic Nothingness)

Sometimes the most productive thing you can do… is absolutely nothing. Not laziness—stillness.

Productivity culture tells us to hustle, grind, and fill every gap with a side hustle. But your brain needs space. Space is where clarity lives.

Taking breaks *on purpose* is a clarity strategy, not a cop-out.

- **Hack 85: Micro-Moments of Stillness**

Once an hour, stop for 60 seconds. No scrolling. No music. Just silence or stillness. Let your brain breathe. You'll be stunned at how much mental power returns.

- **Hack 86: Daydream on Purpose**

Let your mind wander on a walk or while doing dishes. This isn't slacking—it's cognitive composting. Your best ideas often show up when you're not forcing them to.

- **Hack 87: The "Stop Signal" Timer**

Set a timer to go off every 45–60 minutes. When it rings, you pause—no matter what. Stand, stretch, look outside, breathe. It's not about being lazy. It's about avoiding burnout.

- **Hack 88: The 5-5-5 Rule for Brain Clarity**

When overwhelmed, pause and write:

- 5 things you *did* today
- 5 things you're *grateful* for
- 5 things you *don't need to do anymore*

Boom. Clarity, perspective, and release.


## Not the End. Just a Clearer Beginning.

Clarity doesn't come from grinding harder. It comes from removing the static that's in your way.

You don't have to see the entire staircase. You just need to see the next step. And the next sip of water. And the next tab you finally closed. Clarity is built one breath, one pause, one intention at a time.

Brain fog isn't a failure. It's a signal. One that says: slow down, clean up, tune in.

Because the version of you on the other side of that fog?Sharp. Energized. Focused. Ready.

Let's go find them.

# Memory Boosters

## Remember Like a Pro

Memory isn't just about recalling trivia or where you left your sunglasses (though, that too). It's the foundation of learning, problem-solving, decision-making—basically, brain life. When it works, life feels easier. When it's glitchy, everything takes twice as long, and you wonder if you've always been this forgetful or if your brain is now powered by mashed potatoes.

Here's the thing: memory isn't a fixed trait. It's trainable. Sharpenable. You're not stuck with what you've got. With a few mental rewiring tricks, you can make things stick faster, last longer, and show up when you actually need them. This chapter? It's your brain gym. But with less sweat and more "aha!" moments.

We're about to explore simple tools to level up your everyday memory—no flashcards or cram sessions required. Just smart, practical hacks that fit into your life, help things click, and make remembering feel like second nature again.

### Mnemonics That Don't Feel Like Homework

Mnemonics often get a bad rap because they sound like a spelling test—but when done right, they're mental graffiti. Bright. Sticky. Impossible to ignore. Your brain loves patterns, images, and meaning. And if you can make it weird or funny, even better. The more emotional charge, the more memorable the moment.

These aren't school-style memory tricks—they're everyday tools that feel more like mental post-it notes than test prep.

- **Hack 89: Story Glue**

Turn facts into a wild mini-story. Need to remember your shopping list? A banana rides a skateboard into a lake of milk while shouting "EGGS!" You'll never forget it—because your brain can't resist a bizarre tale.

- **Hack 90: Letter Link Chains**

Use the first letters of a series of words to create something wacky. Example: Plan, Act, Track, Think = "Peter Ate Ten Tacos." Make it nonsense. Nonsense = sticky.

- **Hack 91: Personality Mnemonics**

Assign personality traits to what you're trying to remember. "The cautious carrot avoids the reckless radish." Sounds odd? Exactly. Your brain will save it just because it's weird.

- **Hack 92: Rhyme It Till It Sticks**

"If it rhymes, it climbs." Want to remember the steps in a process? Turn them into a little rhyme or chant. Bonus points if it sounds like something from a kid's cartoon.

- **Hack 93: Reverse Mnemonics**

Make up a purposely wrong version of a classic mnemonic—something absurd or unexpected. That contrast helps your brain hang on to the right one. For example, twist "Every Good Boy Deserves Fudge" into "Fat Dogs Bark Every Game." The sillier the switch-up, the stickier the memory.

## The Power of "Recall Over Review"

Reviewing notes is fine. But recalling them without peeking? That's where the memory magic happens. Your brain strengthens memory through retrieval—forcing it to search, stumble, and strengthen.

Active recall is like pulling weights for your brain—it builds mental muscle fast and efficiently. The more effort it takes to remember, the deeper it sticks.

- **Hack 94: Paper Quiz Yourself**

Cover your notes. Write everything you remember on a blank page. Then compare. The gaps you find? That's where learning locks in.

- **Hack 95: Flashcard Speed Rounds**

Set a timer. One minute. Flip through flashcards like your brain's on fire. The goal isn't perfect recall—it's high reps to build fast retrieval.

- **Hack 96: Teach It to a Teddy**

Explain the concept out loud to an imaginary (or real) audience—your cat, a teddy bear, your reflection. Teaching forces deeper encoding.

- **Hack 97: One-Liner Summaries**

After learning something, challenge yourself to sum it up in *one* sentence. Boil it down. If you can't simplify it, you haven't memorized it.

- **Hack 98: Time-Lag Recall**

Review the same info several times, but with growing gaps in between—like once an hour, then the next day, then a few days later. This spaced-out approach tells your brain, "Hey, this matters," and strengthens recall better than cramming.

## Memory Palaces, Chunking, and Anchor Words

These might sound like brainy Hogwarts tricks, but they're actually rooted in cognitive science. Your brain stores information better when it has *places*, *categories*, and *anchors*.

Using structure and spatial imagination helps your brain organize data like a well-labeled filing cabinet. It's not just about memory—it's about making your thoughts easier to find when you need them most.

- **Hack 99: Build a Memory Palace**

Picture a familiar place—like your home—and mentally "store" items you need to remember in different rooms. For example, bananas in the bathtub, a stapler on the couch. Later, take a mental walk through your space to recall each item. It's spatial memory at work.

- **Hack 100: The Rule of 3 (or 4)**

Your brain prefers bite-sized info. Break down long lists into smaller groups of 3 or 4. It's easier to store "Plan / Prepare / Execute" than a messy dozen ungrouped steps. Think in mini-sets.

- **Hack 101: Anchor It to the Familiar**

Trying to learn something new? Link it to something you already know. "This app works like my old Excel sheets, but fancier." Familiarity speeds recall.

- **Hack 102: Visual Labels for Lists**

Give each item in your mental list a bold visual icon. Don't just think "bread, cheese, apples"—think a loaf moonwalking, a cheese disco ball, and an apple doing push-ups.

- **Hack 103: Place = Memory Trigger**

Associate ideas with places you visit often. "Remember to call mom when I reach the coffee shop." Environmental cues can activate stored memories.

## Visualization Tricks for Mental Stickiness

Your brain is a visual beast. If you want something to stick, see it—don't just say it. Abstract concepts become memorable when you attach them to images, motion, and color.

The more senses you involve, the more hooks your memory has to grab onto. Add a little exaggeration, humor, or absurdity, and suddenly, even the boring stuff becomes unforgettable.

- **Hack 104: Mind-Movie Mode**

Create a mini movie scene in your head for what you're trying to remember. Need to recall the 5 stages of something? Act them out like a bizarre film.

- **Hack 105: Color Code Everything**

Use color (real or imagined) to categorize thoughts. Red = urgent. Blue = reference. Yellow = action. Color boosts memory and helps pattern recognition.

- **Hack 106: Symbolic Sketches**

Draw little doodles or symbols for ideas you want to recall. Doesn't have to be good art. Just symbolic enough to jog memory. Your brain loves decoding.

- **Hack 107: Turn Facts into Faces**

Give abstract ideas a human twist—turn them into characters. For example, imagine "Inflation" as a grumpy balloon seller slowly jacking up prices. The more cartoonish, the more your brain latches onto it.

- **Hack 108: Slide Show Snapshot**

As you learn something new, pause and imagine it like a slide in a presentation—frozen mid-moment, bold and bright. This simple mental screenshot slows your brain just enough to tag the info before it slips away.

## Everyday Brain Reps

Just like your muscles need regular movement, so does your memory. You don't have to sit and study—just train your brain to *notice*, *label*, and *retrieve* in daily life.

These micro-movements of memory keep your brain agile, alert, and ready for anything. The goal isn't perfection—it's consistent, playful training that builds recall without the pressure.

- **Hack 109: Name Echo**

When someone tells you their name, use it immediately in conversation. "Nice to meet you, Sam." Then again. It's a micro-rep that burns it into your short-term memory.

- **Hack 110: Object Relocation Recall**

Deliberately place an everyday object—like your keys or charger—in a new spot each day. Then later, try to remember where. It's a mini memory drill that turns your daily routine into a recall challenge.

- **Hack 111: Morning List Recall**

Each morning, try recalling your to-do list or schedule *before* checking your phone. Then compare. It's a way to stretch your memory first thing.

- **Hack 112: Word of the Day Recall**

Pick a random word each day. Challenge yourself to use it in a conversation or write it down in a sentence by the end of the day. New words = new neurons firing.

- **Hack 113: Visual Recall Walks**

On your next walk, observe five things in detail (the color of a door, a license plate, a weird mailbox). When you return, list them. This trains attention *and* memory.

## Your Memory Mission, Complete

Your memory isn't broken—it just hasn't been trained in a while. Like a slightly rusty bike, it's still perfectly functional once you get it moving. These hacks aren't about becoming a trivia robot or memorizing the phone book (do people still do that?). They're about making your brain a better place to store and retrieve what actually matters to *you*.

Whether it's remembering someone's name, retaining new knowledge, or recalling where you parked—memory is a superpower worth sharpening. And lucky for you, it's trainable. No cape required.

Next up: we're clearing out your mental browser history. Brain detox, coming right up.

# Emotional Regulation

## Don't Let Your Brain Hijack You

Ever feel like your brain stages a full-blown emotional takeover without warning? One moment you're calm, the next you're spiraling because of a comment, a glance, or a traffic jam. That's not a character flaw—it's your brain doing its survival dance. The problem? It's dancing to a beat you didn't choose.

Emotional regulation is the art (and science) of not getting steamrolled by your own reactions. It's the skill of pausing mid-freak-out, assessing the storm, and steering your ship—not just clinging to the mast. The good news? You don't need to become a Zen master. You just need a few mental jiu-jitsu moves to calm the chaos and regain control.

This chapter is your emergency toolkit. Whether you're stuck in a thought spiral, melting under pressure, or snapping at someone who just asked a simple question, you'll find hacks that bring your brain back online. Let's tame the inner hijacker.

### Stop, Drop, and Reframe: Thought Loops 101

You know the loop. Something bugs you, and your brain starts circling it like a vulture: *"What if they think I'm a failure?"* *"Why do I always do this?"* *"I can't deal with this right now."* Round and round we go. Thought loops love to turn a single worry into a Broadway-level production of "Everything Is Terrible."

This is your amygdala yelling louder than your logic. The trick? Step out of the loop and into observation mode. Interrupt the pattern. Break the automatic. Replace judgment with curiosity.

- **Hack 114: Give Your Thought a Silly Voice**

Imagine your inner critic speaking in a cartoon voice or with a mouthful of marshmallows. Ridiculous? Exactly. Humor deactivates intensity and helps you detach from the message.

- **Hack 115: "This Is Just a Thought" Trick**

When a thought keeps looping, repeat: "This is just a thought, not a prophecy." It sounds simple, but saying it out loud creates distance between you and the mental noise.

- **Hack 116: Name the Thought Gremlin**

Give your recurring negative thought a ridiculous nickname. "There goes Drama Debbie again." Labeling it makes it feel less like truth and more like an annoying character you don't have to take seriously.

- **Hack 117: "Zoom Out" Camera Lens**

Mentally picture zooming out on your current moment. What does this look like from 30,000 feet? A day from now? A year? It helps shrink the drama and reminds your brain that this is temporary.

- **Hack 118: Run the 'What If' All the Way Out**

Instead of avoiding the thought, complete it. "What if I fail this presentation?"     "Then I'll learn. Maybe I'll improve. Life goes on." Facing the monster often shrinks it.

## Breathing Hacks That Calm Chaos Fast

Breathing: the one thing we all do... badly, when stressed. Your nervous system is more attuned to your breath than to your thoughts. If your breathing says "emergency," your brain believes it.

The magic isn't in *just* breathing—but in how you do it. Slow, conscious breaths reset your internal alarm system and give your thinking brain a seat at the table again.

- **Hack 119: The 4-7-8 Reset**

Inhale for 4, hold for 7, exhale for 8. It's a nervous system lullaby. Great for sleep, anxiety, or that moment before hitting 'Send.'

- **Hack 120: Box Breathing for Brain Clarity**

Breathe in for 4, hold for 4, out for 4, hold for 4. Picture a square in your mind as you go. Navy SEALs use this under pressure. You can use it before answering that tricky email.

- **Hack 121: The Physiological Sigh**

Two short inhales through the nose, one long exhale through the mouth. It mimics your body's natural reset after crying—and it works fast.

- **Hack 122: Finger Breathing**

Trace your finger up as you inhale, down as you exhale. Do this slowly across all five fingers. A tactile + breath combo that calms you with focus.

- **Hack 123: Breathing with Movement**

Pair breathing with a small motion—like rolling your shoulders, wiggling your fingers, or tapping your foot. It grounds you in your body and boosts regulation.

## The Ice Cube Trick (and Other Sensory Resets)

Sometimes your brain doesn't need a motivational speech. It needs a *jolt*. A sensory reset clears emotional fog by activating your physical senses and rebooting your system back into the present.

This isn't woo-woo—it's neuroscience. Intense sensations shift your attention and bring your mind back from the spiral.

- **Hack 124: The Ice Cube Grab**

Hold an ice cube in your hand for 30 seconds. It's safe, cold, and pulls you out of panic mode fast. Bonus: it's oddly grounding.

- **Hack 125: Tense and Release Blitz**

Clench your fists, hold tight for five seconds, then release. Repeat with shoulders, feet, and even your jaw. You'll be surprised how much tension was on autopilot.

- **Hack 126: 5-4-3-2-1 Grounding Game**

Name 5 things you can see, 4 you can touch, 3 you can hear, 2 you can smell, 1 you can taste (or wish you could). It's a sensory scavenger hunt that grounds you in reality.

- **Hack 127: Wrist Splash Trick**

Run cold water over your wrists or splash your face. Quick, accessible, and sends a chill message to your fight-or-flight system: "Stand down."

- **Hack 128: Strong Scent Grounding**

Carry a little bottle of peppermint, citrus, or eucalyptus oil. One sniff can cut through brain fog or panic and jolt you back to the present.

- **Hack 129: Tapping Reset (EFT Lite)**

Tap gently on your collarbone, forehead, or side of your hand while repeating "I'm okay." The rhythm and physical cue create calm through sensory reassurance.

## The Mood Buffer Routine

You can't prevent every emotional storm. But you *can* increase your resilience before it hits. Mood buffering is like emotional sunscreen—it doesn't block every hit, but it helps you burn less.

By stacking small positive habits into your day, you train your brain to return to baseline more quickly, even when life throws a curveball.

- **Hack 130: Pre-Decide Your Exit Plan**

Before you enter a triggering space (like a tough meeting), decide: "If I start spiraling, I'll step out, breathe, or text myself a reminder." Having a plan shrinks the power of the unknown.

- **Hack 131: One-Song Reset**

Pick a single go-to song that shifts your mood. Play it loud. Dance, cry, yell—whatever helps move the emotion through. One song is often enough.

- **Hack 132: The Bookend Buffer**

Start and end your day with intention—even if it's just 2 minutes. Light a candle, stretch, journal a line. This creates a soft emotional landing and lift-off.

- **Hack 133: Ask Future You**

Before reacting, ask: "What would 'me in 3 hours' wish I'd done?" Future You is often wiser and calmer. Borrow their perspective.

- **Hack 134: The "10-Minute Favor" Rule**

Do one small thing, your future self will thank you for—clean a corner, prep a meal, reply to a nagging message. It builds a sense of control and progress.

- **Hack 135: 3-Minute Sunshine Snack**

Step outside for 3 minutes of fresh air and sun (even if it's cloudy). Light regulates mood and energy fast. Bonus: Take your shoes off if there's grass nearby.

- **Hack 136: Micro-Wins Tracker**

At the end of the day, jot down 2–3 things you did that made progress—even if tiny. Wins stack up and signal your brain that today mattered.

## Journaling for Brains That Don't Want to Journal

You don't need to be the "Dear Diary" type to benefit from journaling. Even reluctant writers can unlock clarity with the right prompt. This isn't about crafting essays—it's about brain-dumping the chaos out of your head and onto paper.

Journaling is a pressure-release valve for thoughts that swirl too long. It gives form to the fuzzy and lets you see patterns before they become problems.

- **Hack 137: One Line a Day**

Too tired to write? Just do one line. "Today was…" That's it. Consistency matters more than depth. Over time, even one-liners tell a powerful story.

- **Hack 138: The Emotional Debrief**

Ask yourself: "What am I feeling, and why?" Write without censoring. The act of labeling emotion is a calming force in itself.

- **Hack 139: Scribble the Storm**

Set a timer for 3 minutes. Scribble everything on your mind—rants, lists, nonsense. Then stop. Don't reread it. It's not for analysis—it's for unloading.

- **Hack 140: Journal to a Person (Real or Imaginary)**

Write a note to someone—your future self, a mentor, a cartoon character. This helps you step outside your head and gain new angles.

- **Hack 141: Gratitude with Grit**

Instead of "I'm grateful for sunshine," write one gritty, real gratitude: "I'm grateful I didn't yell when the meeting crashed again." The more specific, the more powerful.

## Your Calm Is a Skill

Emotions are not enemies—they're messengers. But when they shout, hijack, or overstay their welcome, we need tools to guide them gently back to the sidelines. You don't have to suppress your feelings to stay calm. You just have to learn how to respond instead of react.

With a few strategic mental shortcuts, you can go from meltdown to manageable, chaos to clarity. The goal isn't perfect emotional control—it's better recovery, faster bounce-backs, and fewer spirals.

Next time your brain tries to hijack the wheel, smile, grab your hacks, and say, "Nice try, but I've got this."

# Mindfulness Without the Woo

## Calm, Clear, and Grounded

Mindfulness has a branding problem. It sounds like you need a meditation cushion, an ocean soundtrack, and a daily yoga practice to qualify. Spoiler alert: you don't.

At its core, mindfulness is just training your brain to notice. Notice your thoughts. Notice your body. Notice when you're spiraling so you can hit pause instead of panic. It's not about becoming a serene monk — it's about not losing your cool when life hits weird.

This chapter will give you **low-effort, zero-woo strategies** to build calm into your brain's default operating system — in between meetings, on the train, or while washing your face.

### What Mindfulness Really Means (No Robes Required)

Mindfulness is not the art of clearing your mind like a Zen master. It's the skill of *seeing* your thoughts without instantly believing or reacting to them. Think of it like opening 20 browser tabs in your brain... but only clicking on the one that actually matters.

When you're mindful, you're not trying to "stop thinking." You're just becoming the boss of which thought you follow, and which one gets closed before it crashes the system.

- **Hack 142: The Thought Traffic Hack**

Picture your thoughts as cars passing on a road. You don't have to chase everyone. Just notice: "Ah, anxious thought passing by." Let it keep driving. You're standing on the sidewalk, not in the middle of the street.

- **Hack 143: Mental Weather Report**

Instead of identifying *with* your mood, observe it like the weather. "There's a storm of frustration today." You're not *angry* — there's *anger*. It's passing through, not who you are. Labeling this way gives you mental distance without needing a cartoon name.

- **Hack 144: The "I Noticed" Journal**

Once a day, jot down one thing you noticed *in the moment* — a sound, a sensation, a thought before it ran wild. It trains the mindfulness muscle subtly.

- **Hack 145: Label It, Don't Judge It**

When you catch a tough emotion, don't wrestle it. Just name it: "I'm feeling tense." That simple act shifts you from swimming in it to standing beside it.

- **Hack 146: The 10-Second Wait Trick**

Feel like reacting? Wait 10 seconds. Just long enough to give your wiser brain a chance to step in. It's like hitting snooze on the impulse.

- **Hack 147: Default Mode Disruptor**

Your brain's default mode network loves to daydream or worry. Disrupt it once an hour by simply noticing your breath, body, or surroundings. It's like tapping your brain on the shoulder and saying, "Hey, we're here now."

## Micro-Meditation (1–2 Minute Resets for Real Life)

You don't need to sit cross-legged for 20 minutes to get the benefits of meditation. Micro-meditations — quick, intentional moments of stillness — can refresh your brain mid-chaos without needing a retreat center.

These are realistic for actual humans, not monks. Think of them as mental mouthwash. Swish, breathe, move on.

- **Hack 148: Sigh Cycle Reset**

Breathe in gently through your nose. Then exhale with a loud audible *sigh*. Repeat this 3 times. That exaggerated sigh isn't just drama — it stimulates your vagus nerve and helps offload mental pressure like steam from a kettle.

- **Hack 149: The One-Breath Pause**

Before opening an email, entering a room, or answering a question — take one full breath. It adds a sliver of space between input and reaction.

- **Hack 150: 60-Second Stillness**

Set a timer for 1 minute. Sit, close your eyes, and do nothing but breathe. Your brain will scream to check your phone. Don't. This is the point.

- **Hack 151: Guided Voice Shortcuts**

Save a couple of 1–3 minute guided meditations on your phone. Use them when you're stuck, spiraling, or zoning out. No shame in borrowing someone else's calm.

- **Hack 152: Hand on Heart Check-In**

Place your hand over your heart, close your eyes, and say: "I'm here." Sounds cheesy. Works every time.

- **Hack 153: Micro Zen Stretch**

Stand up. Reach for the ceiling. Breathe. Drop your arms slowly. Feel the floor under your feet. Takes 15 seconds. Resets your system.

## Get Out of Your Head and Into Your Senses

When your thoughts go haywire — racing, looping, or spiraling — your senses are your secret weapon. Tuning into the physical world helps interrupt mental static. It's not about suppressing your emotions; it's about shifting gears so you can respond, not just react.

Sensory hacks give your brain a safe exit ramp. They bring you back to "here and now" without needing a therapist or a yoga mat. Just your body, your surroundings, and a few moments of attention.

- **Hack 154: The Tactile Grounder**

Keep a textured object (stone, fabric, keyring) in your pocket. When you feel overwhelmed, hold it and describe its texture in detail. Touch brings you home.

- **Hack 155: The Color Hunt**

Pick a color. Find five things in the room that match it. Simple visual focus that breaks the loop of runaway thoughts.

- **Hack 156: Barefoot Reconnect**

Step outside and place your bare feet on grass, tile, or dirt. Even a minute of grounding this way can reduce mental noise.

- **Hack 157: Name the Sounds Game**

Pause and list every sound you can hear right now — even the faint ones. Gets your brain out of your head and into your ears.

- **Hack 158: The Texture Scan**

Run your hand across different surfaces: desk, fabric, your skin, your cup. Describe how each one feels — smooth, warm, rough, cold. It's sensory anchoring, not just fidgeting.

## Breathwork, Body Scans & Why They Work

Your breath is a built-in nervous system remote. Use it well, and you can downshift from frantic to functional in seconds. Add body awareness, and you unlock a new level of "oh wow, I didn't even know I was clenching my butt."

Body scans and breathwork aren't new-age fluff. They're backed by science and used by elite athletes, therapists, and trauma experts alike.

- **Hack 159: The Coffee Stir Breath**

Breathe in through your nose as if smelling your favorite coffee. Hold briefly. Then exhale slowly through pursed lips like you're cooling a hot drink. Repeat 3 times. This visualization softens your breath, body, and thoughts.

- **Hack 160: 3-Point Body Scan**

Focus your attention on three areas: forehead, shoulders, and stomach. Ask, "Can I soften here?" This mini scan reduces tension fast.

- **Hack 161: Diaphragm Check-In**

Put one hand on your chest and one on your belly. Breathe. Try to move the belly hand more than the chest hand. This activates calmer breathing patterns.

- **Hack 162: Jaw Dropper Reset**

Clench your jaw and release it slowly. Repeat 3 times. Most of us hold stress in our faces — even when we're "resting."

- **Hack 163: Progressive Squeeze & Breathe**

Squeeze your toes, hold, release. Then your calves. Then thighs. All the way up to your face. Pair with deep breathing. It's like a mental massage.

- **Hack 164: Vagus Nerve Vibe**

Humming, chanting, or even singing triggers your vagus nerve. Which is science-speak for: it helps you chill.

## Use the Shower for Mental Clarity (aka, the Wet Zen Hack)

Ever notice how your best ideas come in the shower? There's a reason for that. Your brain switches to diffuse mode when you're relaxed and unstimulated — aka standing under warm water doing nothing important.

But it's more than just creative sparks. The shower can become your **daily brain rinse**, both literally and emotionally.

- **Hack 165: "Wash Off the Day" Visual**

As the water hits you, imagine it rinsing off stress, noise, and pressure. It's a mental reset disguised as hygiene.

- **Hack 166: Shower Breathe-Down**

Inhale deeply as the water runs over you. Exhale slowly. Match breath to water rhythm. It creates an easy meditative flow — no effort needed.

- **Hack 167: Wet Affirmation Ritual**

Pick one positive statement like "I'm safe," "I'm capable," or "I'm resetting." Repeat it three times aloud while rinsing. It anchors the thought with sensory input.

- **Hack 168: Cold-Then-Warm Wake-Up**

End your shower with 15 seconds of cold, then switch to warm. The contrast jolts your nervous system into a state of alert calm — a weirdly effective response.

- **Hack 169: Shampoo Mantra Hack**

While shampooing or soaping up, repeat a calming phrase in your head. It gives your busy brain a job that isn't worrying.

- **Hack 170: Post-Shower Stillness**

Before rushing off, sit or stand for one minute while drying. No phone. No rushing. Just notice how your body feels now. That moment is mindfulness.

## The Calm Is Already In You

You don't need to download a mindfulness app, buy a yoga mat, or fly to Bali to access stillness. It's already built into your system. The trick is learning to spot the noise, press pause, and give your nervous system a breather.

Mindfulness isn't about perfection or peace that lasts forever. It's about *noticing when you've left the moment* — and gently coming back. Again and again.

So whether you're standing in line, stuck in traffic, or scrubbing shampoo into your hair — you've got options. Little hacks, big shifts.

Next time your mind starts to spin, don't try to escape it.

Just look it in the eye and say, "I'm here. Let's breathe."

# Cognitive Flexibility

## Bounce Back, Think Different

Your brain is a pattern-detecting machine. It loves routine, predictability, and things that make sense. But life isn't always so cooperative. Sometimes, things go sideways, expectations crumble, or you find yourself stuck in a loop of rigid thinking—convinced there's only one right way, one solution, or one version of the truth.

Enter cognitive flexibility.

This isn't about being indecisive or flaky. It's the opposite. Flexibility means you can adapt without unraveling, bounce back without denying reality, and see new angles without abandoning logic. It's how you stay creative under pressure, problem-solve when things change, and break free from the mental ruts that hold you back.

You're not trying to force a silver lining or slap a smiley face on real frustration. You're building the ability to **shift perspective**—to zoom out, turn the problem upside down, and ask, "What else might be true?" The more you practice it, the faster you get at snapping out of tunnel vision and stepping into possibility.

Let's stretch those mental muscles.

### Mindset Shifting Made Easy (and funny)

You don't need a life coach or a spiritual retreat to shift your mindset. Sometimes, all it takes is a nudge—a tiny invitation to see things differently. Humor, curiosity, and reframing aren't about pretending the hard stuff doesn't exist. They're about choosing a different lens when the current one makes everything look impossible.

Let's make your mindset more flexible—without losing your mind.

- **Hack 171: The Potato Theory**

Whatever you're panicking about, imagine explaining it to a potato. If the potato didn't care, maybe it's not worth your emotional bandwidth. Oddly grounding.

- **Hack 172: The Alternate Universe Answer**

Imagine your current perspective came from a parallel universe version of you — the one who always expects the worst. Now, write the response from another you in a *better* universe. This isn't fantasy — it's permission to try on optimism without the pressure to believe it yet.

- **Hack 173: Opposite Day Mode**

Ask yourself: "If I believed the *opposite* of this thought, how would I behave?" Example: Instead of "I'm terrible at this," try "I'm capable, even if I'm learning." Act from that belief and see what changes.

- **Hack 174: Third-Person Perspective Swap**

Narrate your current struggle in the third person. "Taylor is having a hard week. They feel like everything is off track, but they've handled worse." Research shows that talking about yourself this way creates emotional distance and greater clarity. It's weirdly powerful.

- **Hack 175: Flip the Frame**

Take a frustrating moment and give it a new headline like it's a news story. "Disaster at Work" becomes "Learning Curve in Progress.""Awkward Date" becomes "Comedy Night: Starring Me."Humor disarms defensiveness. Reframing doesn't deny reality — it just rewrites the script to one you want to keep reading.

## Scenario Swapping: The Improv Brain Trick

Improvisation actors train their brains to respond with "Yes, and…" instead of freezing or fighting a new situation. You can borrow that approach to unlock better reactions and new solutions. When something goes wrong, instead of spiraling, you can think like an improv master: What *else* could I say? What *else* could happen?

It's a brain gym for possibility—and it's sneakily fun.

- **Hack 176: Play the Role**

Act as if you're someone else facing this situation. How would Detective You, Artist You, or Explorer You handle it? Channel a different mindset to unlock new ideas.

- **Hack 177: Opposite Action Practice**

Your brain expects you to react a certain way. Surprise it. If you usually shut down when embarrassed, try initiating a conversation. If you always say no to something new, say yes just once. Opposite actions create neural flexibility. You're not betraying yourself — you're expanding what "you" can mean.

- **Hack 178: Alternate Endings**

Imagine three totally different outcomes for the same situation—wild, boring, or surprising. You're training your brain not to lock in on one path as "the truth."

- **Hack 179: Yes, And... Your Inner Voice**

Instead of shutting down a feeling ("This is stupid"), say "Yes, and..." Example: "Yes, I'm nervous, and I've done harder things before." You're allowing emotion but adding momentum.

## Reframing Failure (it's not toxic positivity, promise)

Failure isn't the end. It's data. It's feedback. It's how humans learn—awkwardly and in public. But your brain doesn't always agree. It often treats any misstep like a full-system crash.

Reframing failure is about giving your brain a new story: not one where you failed, but one where you experimented, learned, and adjusted. You're not ignoring reality—you're building resilience inside it.

- **Hack 180: The Failure Folder**

Keep a private document or journal where you record failures—but only *after* listing what they taught you. It turns flops into a highlight reel of growth.

- **Hack 181: Zoom in on the Effort, Not the Outcome**

Instead of obsessing over what didn't work, ask: What did I try that was brave? Where did I show up? Focus on *what you controlled*.

- **Hack 182: The Scientist Reframe**

Imagine you're a researcher. That last thing you tried? It was one iteration of an experiment. "Interesting result," you say. "What's the next version?"

- **Hack 183: Write the Failure Résumé**

Make a fake résumé that lists jobs you didn't get, ideas that flopped, and lessons you earned the hard way. Wear it like a badge of evolution, not shame.

## The "What Else Could Be True?" Technique

Rigid thinking loves certainty. "This always happens." "They don't like me." "I'm not good enough." The brain latches on to these stories like they're hard facts.

This hack cracks that open. It invites your brain to play detective, not judge. You're not forcing optimism—you're making room for *more than one* possible truth.

- **Hack 184: Run the Reality Scan**

Write your thoughts. Then ask: What's the proof *for* this? What's the proof *against* it? What's a neutral explanation? Just like a courtroom—it forces your brain to think in layers.

- **Hack 185: Try the "Other Shoes" Game**

Mentally walk through the situation from 3 different perspectives: yours, theirs, and an outsider's. The goal isn't to excuse—it's to expand your frame.

- **Hack 186: The 10% Shift**

Ask: "What's *one part* of this thought that might be wrong, exaggerated, or missing context?" You don't need a total rewrite. Just a crack of doubt opens space for balance.

- **Hack 187: Break One Rule (On Purpose)**

Sometimes, mental agility starts with gently loosening your grip on "the way things *should* be." Pick one low-stakes expectation you typically follow — and choose to bend it. Eat breakfast *after* the to-do list. Wear mismatched socks. Speak up when you'd usually stay quiet. It's not about being reckless. It's about reminding your brain it has options — that not all structure is sacred.

- **Hack 188: Outsource the Thought**

Say your thought aloud as if it came from someone else. "My friend thinks she's a failure because of one awkward meeting." What would you say to her?

## Reverse Brainstorming

Your brain is great at solving problems—but it's even better at *creating* them. Reverse brainstorming flips your mental engine upside down to find unexpected answers. Instead of asking, "How do I fix this?" you ask, "How could I make this worse?" Weirdly, it works.

Once your brain gets silly and extreme, it often reveals exactly where the real fix is hiding.

- **Hack 189: Worst-Case Builder**

Ask yourself: "If I wanted to absolutely sabotage this situation, what would I do?" List at least five bad ideas. Then reverse-engineer them into your action plan.

- **Hack 190: Anti-Productivity Hour**

Spend 10 minutes imagining how to be completely unproductive today. Then do the opposite. Clarity through contrast.

- **Hack 191: Advice to Your Worst Enemy**

If you wanted someone to fail, what advice would you give them? Now ask: Am I actually doing any of that myself?

- **Hack 192: Backwards Goal Map**

Take your goal and work backwards by identifying every step that would guarantee failure. Then flip each one to find your real to-do list.

**Let's Twist Again**

Cognitive flexibility isn't about being endlessly cheerful or ignoring reality. It's about mental movement — the ability to shift, pivot, and reframe without snapping in two.It's about asking: *"Is this the only way to see this?"* instead of clinging to the first story your brain throws at you.

Every time you switch perspectives, entertain a new possibility, or soften a rigid belief, you're not just thinking differently — you're training your brain to bend instead of break.

So the next time you feel mentally gridlocked, try this:Pause. Breathe. Tilt your head a little.What else could be true here? What would a more flexible version of you say?

Your brain's not stuck. It's just waiting for a twist.Let the pivot begin.

# Brain-Friendly Routines
## Outsmart Yourself

You don't need a personality transplant to stick to better habits. You don't need to "try harder" or "just be consistent." In fact, most of what we've been told about routines is somewhat backward. Habits don't fail because you're lazy — they fail because they weren't designed for the way your brain actually works. Your brain isn't wired for relentless willpower. It's wired for ease, for shortcuts, and for whatever feels good in the moment.

You're not broken because you keep falling off the wagon — you're human. And your brain is doing what it was built to do: avoid discomfort, seek rewards, and conserve energy. So instead of fighting that, what if we worked with it? This chapter isn't about waking up at 5 a.m. or powering through your to-do list. It's about creating flexible systems that run in the background — the kind that hold up even when you're tired, distracted, or hangry and your inbox is vomiting chaos.

We're going to build habits that feel natural, not forced. Routines that are anchored in your real life — not your fantasy life. The goal here isn't discipline. Its design. You're not here to win the willpower Olympics. You're here to outsmart yourself — in the best possible way.

### Why Habits Fail (Spoiler: It's Not Your Willpower)

Habits don't usually fail because you're lazy. They fail because the system you built was too vague, too hard, or too disconnected from your real life. Willpower is a limited, glitchy battery. If your habits rely on it alone, they're already set up to crumble under stress. And when life throws curveballs (as it always does), your habits shouldn't be the first thing to break.

Let's redesign from the inside out.

- **Hack 193: Don't "Add" — Replace**

Instead of saying "I need to stop checking my phone," say "When I feel the urge, I'll do X instead." Replacing is easier than removing.

- **Hack 194: Create a Habit Graveyard**

Make a list of habits you tried but didn't stick with — the ones that quietly fizzled out or crashed hard. Now do a little forensic work: What caused each one to fail? Was it too boring? Too inconvenient? Too vague? Each "failed" habit leaves a clue. When you understand why they didn't last, you can design new ones that actually will.

- **Hack 195: Willpower Budget**

Think of your self-control like a wallet with limited cash. Don't blow it on small stuff like debating whether to floss or do five pushups. Automate the simple things, so you have energy left for the big, messy decisions that actually matter.

- **Hack 196: Stop Aiming for 100%**

Your brain hates perfection. Let 80% be the new perfect. That 20% wiggle room keeps shame out of the driver's seat.

- **Hack 197: Shrink the Commitment**

Make the habit laughably easy. "Stretch for 2 minutes" instead of "Do 30 minutes of yoga." Small sticks better.

## Cue > Craving > Response > Reward – The Real Habit Loop

Habits aren't just routines — they're loops your brain runs on autopilot. First comes a cue, then a craving, then a response, and finally a reward. Break or tweak just one part, and the whole loop shifts. That's the real lever for change — not grit, but smarter inputs.

Most people try to bulldoze the behavior without ever examining what triggered it in the first place. If you don't know the cue or the craving, you're swinging in the dark.

Let's tinker with the wiring.

- **Hack 198: Create a Specific Cue**

Tie your habit to something real and repeating: brushing teeth, starting the kettle, turning on the light.

- **Hack 199: Stack a Reward Immediately**

Don't wait for "eventual benefits." Give your brain a dopamine hit now. Think: checking a box, listening to a favorite song, or even a celebratory fist pump. Small pleasures seal the loop.

- **Hack 200: If-Then Looping**

Build mental shortcuts with simple formulas: "If X happens, then I do Y." Example: "If I finish lunch, then I stretch." This rewires your brain for auto-action.

- **Hack 201: Visualize the Craving**

Before responding to the habit loop, pause and visualize the craving. Ask: "What am I *really* craving right now?" Sometimes it's not the snack or scroll—it's rest, relief, or connection in disguise.

- **Hack 202: Interrupt the Pattern Physically**

Stand up. Change rooms. Clap your hands. Moving your body breaks auto-mode and buys you a microsecond to choose better.

## The 2-Minute Gate – Short Habits That Unlock Long Ones

The biggest lie habits tell you? That you have to "feel ready" first. Spoiler: You won't. But you *can* lower the entry fee.

Enter the 2-minute gate — a brain hack that says, "You don't have to do *all* the things. Just the first 2 minutes of it." The magic? Most of the time, you'll keep going anyway. But even if you don't, you've still won. You showed up.

- **Hack 203: Floss One Tooth**

If that's all you do, that's enough. This trains your identity, not just your enamel.

- **Hack 204: The Sock Rule**

Want to work out? Step one is putting on your gym socks. If you still don't feel like it after that, you're off the hook.

- **Hack 205: 2-Minute Writing Sprint**

Set a 2-minute timer. Write anything. The brain can't resist finishing a sentence once it starts.

- **Hack 206: Micro-Move Your Goalposts**

Break the habit down until it's laughably doable. Can't read a chapter? Open the book and read one sentence.

- **Hack 207: Stack the Tiny Win**

Each 2-minute habit you complete stacks proof that you're the kind of person who shows up — and that identity shift is gold.

## The Power of Visual Reminders

Out of sight, out of mind is painfully real. Visual cues are like gentle brain nudges: "Hey, remember me?" They bring intention back into view — even when your brain is busy, tired, or halfway through a doom scroll.

Want to stick to a habit? Make it impossible to ignore. Let's make your habits visible.

- **Hack 208: Leave It Out**

Want to journal? Leave the notebook open on your pillow. Want to drink water? Put the bottle on your keyboard.

- **Hack 209: Habit Boards**

Use a whiteboard, sticky note grid, or calendar tracker that you see daily. Not for guilt — for guidance.

- **Hack 210: Message Mirrors**

Write habit nudges on your mirror: "Breathe. Stretch. Smile." A reminder when you're not doom scrolling.

- **Hack 211: Pre-Set Your Space**

Before bed, lay out your walking shoes or prep the blender. Make the next step frictionless and in-your-face.

## Identity-Based Habits: "I'm the Kind of Person Who..."

Habits stick better when they connect to who you believe you are. Not "I need to run," but "I'm the kind of person who moves daily." Identity isn't just motivation — it's a shortcut to consistency.

If your habit feels like proof of who you are, it becomes easier to keep going. Instead of chasing perfect routines, let's anchor your actions in your identity. Let's shift from doing to being — from effort to alignment.

- **Hack 212: Create a Character Card**

Write a one-line "character description" for your future self — like you're writing a role for a movie. "She's the kind of person who never skips a morning walk." Seeing it written cements the belief.

- **Hack 213: Track Tiny Wins**

Instead of just logging what you did, label each win as identity evidence. "Replied to that tricky email = I'm someone who handles hard things." Keep the focus on *who you're becoming*, not just what you did.

- **Hack 214: Break Up with Old Labels**

Watch out for identity anchors like "I'm just a procrastinator" or "I'm not a math person." Challenge them. Outdated self-labels quietly sabotage action. Rewrite them with possibility, not permanence.

- **Hack 215: Ritual Reinforcement**

Use a tiny closing ritual to reinforce your identity. After writing, say: "That's me — a writer." After a workout: "Still got it." The ritual ties action to self-image.

- **Hack 216: Vote with Your Actions**

Every choice is a ballot. One workout doesn't make you an athlete — but it's a vote. And the more votes you cast, the more confident your brain becomes in your new identity.

## Temptation Bundling

If you can't beat the craving, marry it to something useful. That's temptation bundling — pairing a want with a should-do. It's not cheating. It's strategy. You're hijacking your own reward system to get things done.

Instead of forcing discipline, you're creating a win-win loop your brain actually wants to repeat. The craving stays — but now it's doing your chores.

Let's trade guilt for strategy.

- **Hack 217: Podcast + Chores**

Only let yourself listen to your favorite podcast while folding laundry or walking.

- **Hack 218: Screen Time + Movement**

Watch YouTube only while on a stationary bike or pacing.

- **Hack 219: Coffee + Planning**

Pair your morning caffeine hit with a 2-minute task list brain dump.

- **Hack 220: Netflix + Stretching**

Stretch during the intro credits or scene changes. Entertainment with side benefits.

- **Hack 221: Audiobook While Tidying**

Your brain stops resisting tasks when it's getting a treat.


## The "Bright Lines" Rule

Some habits need flexibility. Others need a firm line in the sand. While soft systems and gradual shifts often work best, there are cases where clarity is king — especially when decision fatigue or slippery temptations get in the way.

Bright lines are simple, non-negotiable rules you define in advance. Not to punish yourself — but to take the daily decision off your plate.

They reduce moral bargaining, strengthen identity, and give your brain a shortcut to "nope."

Let's draw lines with kindness and purpose.

- **Hack 222: "I Don't" Language**

Say "I don't scroll before 9 a.m." vs. "I try not to…" The former is identity-based and firmer.

- **Hack 223: Clear Windows**

Create time boxes: "No work emails after 7 p.m." or "Only snacks between 3–4."

- **Hack 224: All or Nothing (Sometimes)**

For certain habits, total abstinence is easier than moderation. Know which ones need a full block.

- **Hack 225: Externalize the Rule**

Write your rule and post it somewhere visible. Make it public, even if it's just to your fridge.

- **Hack 226: Reward Following the Line**

Every time you stick to your bright line, reward yourself — sticker, check mark, happy dance.


## Make Decisions Once (Not 100x Daily)

Decision fatigue kills motivation. Every tiny choice—what to eat, what to wear, when to work out—slowly drains your willpower. The more options you juggle, the more likely your brain is to default to "meh, maybe later."

Let's stop choosing and start pre-deciding — fewer micro-decisions mean more energy for things that actually matter.

- **Hack 227: Default Meals**

Have go-to breakfasts and lunches. Less drama, more consistency.

- **Hack 228: Outfit Rotation**

Choose 3–5 outfit combos you like and rotate them. Steve Jobs didn't stress about socks.

- **Hack 229: Theme Days**

Assign tasks to days: "Monday = admin, Wednesday = meetings." No more daily juggling.

- **Hack 230: Pre-Planned Play**

Schedule your fun too. "Friday = movie night." Your brain respects blocked joy.

- **Hack 231: Eliminate Tiny Decisions**

Use auto-ship for groceries. Put phone chargers everywhere. Set recurring calendar events.

## Let Your Habits Do the Heavy Lifting

The smartest brain isn't the one that tries harder. It's the one that plans smarter. Routines are your backstage crew — they quietly prep the stage, so you don't need a daily pep talk to show up and perform. They don't drain your willpower; they automate it.

Consistency doesn't come from being more disciplined — it comes from designing systems that work even when you're tired, distracted, or unmotivated. That's the power of letting habits lead the way. They take the burden off your brain and turn effort into autopilot.

So stop blaming yourself when things fall through. You're not broken — your setup is. Redesign it to be kinder, simpler, and harder to break.

Make it easier to win. Not just once, but every day. That's how your future self thrives — not through force, but through strategy.

# Creativity Hacks

## Break the Thought Mold

Your brain is a pattern machine — efficient, fast, and... occasionally stuck in its own loops. That's not a flaw. It's how we survive. But when it comes to creativity — whether it's solving a problem, crafting a message, or dreaming up something new — these patterns can become mental ruts. Real creativity isn't about being struck by sudden genius. It's about disrupting your usual loops and giving your brain space to explore different paths.

This chapter isn't about becoming the next Picasso or writing a bestselling novel overnight. It's about turning the tap back on. Whether your creativity is buried under stress, busyness, or just hasn't been used in a while, these hacks will help you reawaken it. We're going to explore play, music, movement, constraints, and low-pressure ways to let ideas bloom again — not by force, but by design. Because creativity doesn't just show up. You build a playground.

Let's break the mold and reboot your thinking.

### The Brainstorm Warm-Up (Low-Stakes Play)

Great ideas rarely arrive when you're sitting stiffly at your desk, demanding brilliance. Your brain needs a warm-up — a stretch, a joke, a harmless detour — to get into creative mode.

Play isn't the opposite of productivity. It's the gateway. A few minutes of silliness or scribbling can unlock the flow state that pressure locks away. Think of it like cracking your knuckles before lifting the lid off your best ideas.

- **Hack 232: 3-Minute Nonsense List**

Set a timer. Write down the most absurd uses for a spoon. Or 10 imaginary band names. Or new names for clouds. When the stakes are zero, your brain stops filtering.

- **Hack 233: Wrong Answers Only**

Start your brainstorming session by deliberately coming up with terrible ideas. "How *not* to solve this?" It relaxes your inner critic and unlocks lateral thinking.

- **Hack 234: Doodle Before You Think**

Grab a pen and doodle shapes, arrows, or totally abstract nonsense. Doodling lowers inhibition and revs up your visual thinking circuits.

- **Hack 235: Pretend It's Not You**

Ask: "What would a pirate, astronaut, or toddler do with this problem?" Taking on a playful persona dislodges serious mental blocks.

- **Hack 236: Curiosity Before Cleverness**

Before aiming for the smartest solution, list five questions about the challenge. Curiosity is a spark — creativity is what happens when it catches fire.


## Movement + Music = Idea Generation

Sitting still in silence? Creativity's natural enemy. Your brain thrives on rhythm, motion, and sensory stimulation. Think of it as shaking the snow globe. Movement increases blood flow, music boosts dopamine — together, they create the ideal neuro-cocktail for fresh thinking.

So next time you're stuck, don't force it. Walk, dance, bounce, or put on a beat. Ideas like to hitch rides — so move.

- **Hack 237: Walk + Talk**

Record yourself while walking and rambling about the problem. Your mouth often knows more than your pen does. Transcribe later, gold nuggets included.

- **Hack 238: Playlist Priming**

Build playlists that match the emotion you want your idea to evoke. Joyful, eerie, calm, chaotic — the music sets your neural tone.

- **Hack 239: Dance Break Download**

Set a silly timer. When it goes off, blast a song and move your body. This tiny pattern interruption resets your neural circuitry.

- **Hack 240: Beat-Based Thinking**

Use a metronome or drum loop to maintain a steady tempo while you write or sketch. Rhythmic sound nudges your brain into a state of flow faster than silence ever could.

- **Hack 241: Tempo Shift**

Slow song? Gentle ideas. Fast beat? Bold ones. Match your brainstorming session to the energy you want to explore.

- **Hack 242: Sonic Palette Swap**

Work on your idea while switching genres every 5 minutes — jazz, EDM, lo-fi, classical. Each change triggers a mental shift and opens up new creative perspectives.


## White Space = Creative Space

Your brain isn't a warehouse. It's a garden. Cramming every second with inputs kills your ability to compose ideas, form connections, and hear that tiny whisper of inspiration. You need mental breathing room to let scattered thoughts bump into each other and form something new.

Quiet is not wasted time. It's when the magic grows. Silence isn't empty — it's full of possibility.

- **Hack 243: The Nothing Hour**

Schedule an hour with no input. No screens. No podcasts. No to-do lists. Just a notebook and your brain. Let the boredom bloom.

- **Hack 244: Visual Breathing Room**

Clean your workspace. Leave white space in your journal. Your eyes crave calm — clutter crushes cognition.

- **Hack 245: The 20% Rule**

Reserve 20% of your creative time for wandering — mentally or physically. No goals, just space. Your brain will fill it in ways you didn't expect.

- **Hack 246: Input Detox**

Pick one day a week where you consume nothing new: no books, no scrolls, no videos. Let the noise fade and your own thoughts echo back louder.

- **Hack 247: Make Blank Time Sacred**

Treat empty hours like meetings with your future brilliance. Put them on the calendar and defend them fiercely.

## The Constraint Trick: Fewer Options, Better Ideas

Total freedom sounds amazing… until your brain short-circuits. Unlimited possibilities = unlimited paralysis. Your creativity gets lost in the fog of too many choices. But give it a boundary? Suddenly, it knows where to run. Constraints focus your attention, narrow the playground, and force creativity through the squeeze.

Think of them like puzzle edges — they don't limit the picture, they give it shape. Whether it's a time cap, a word limit, or only using what's on your desk, constraints act like a creative spark plug. Boxes aren't barriers. They're launchpads.

- **Hack 248: Use Random Limits**

"Write it in exactly 13 words." "Use only shades of blue." "Only circles, no lines." These silly walls lead to surprising breakthroughs.

- **Hack 249: Half the Resources**

Imagine doing your task with half the time, half the money, or half the tools. Pressure creates diamonds — and better solutions.

- **Hack 250: Time-Locked Ideas**

Set a 7-minute timer and generate ideas until it dings. No edits. No overthinking. Scarcity sharpens focus.

- **Hack 251: Reverse the Rules**

Pick one rule of your task — and break it. Make the serious silly, the short long, the loud quiet. Constraints can be broken too.

- **Hack 252: One Word at a Time**

Trying to write or speak? Limit yourself to one-word sentences for a few minutes. It's awkward. And wildly freeing.

- **Hack 253: Only the Opposite**

Force yourself to write or sketch the *opposite* of what you mean for 5 minutes. By narrowing your direction in reverse, you'll often uncover the heart of the idea.

## Idea Parking Lot (Keep It Flowing, Not Forgotten)

Good ideas rarely arrive on schedule. If you don't capture them, they vanish. If you try to use them all at once, you'll overload. Your brain isn't built to juggle everything at once — it needs a shelf, not a spotlight.

Your best thinking isn't always for now. But it's definitely not for never. You need a middle ground — a creative holding zone.

- **Hack 254: Idea Inbox**

Use a single place (physical or digital) to dump every new thought. No categories. No filters. Just catch them before they float away.

- **Hack 255: The Swipe File**

Collect things that spark you: ads, headlines, photos, quotes, napkin scribbles. Keep them organized by vibe, not topic. This is your creative compost bin.

- **Hack 256: Icebox Review Day**

Set aside one day a month to dig through your parking lot. Sort, combine, discard. Let your past self surprise you.

- **Hack 257: Half-Idea Heaven**

Don't wait for perfect ideas. Park the half-baked ones too. Some of your weirdest fragments will grow into brilliance with time.

- **Hack 258: Parking Lot Prompts**

Turn parked ideas into prompts: "What would make this idea useful?" or "What does this remind me of?" Use questions to unlock the next layer.

- **Hack 259: Idea "Mood Tags"**

When parking an idea, tag it with a mood or color — "Exciting," "Needs courage," "Weird but funny." These emotional markers make it easier to return and build later

## Catch It, Don't Crash It - Creative Cross-Pollination

Great ideas often come from unexpected combinations — not lightning bolts. Borrowing concepts from one domain and applying them to another creates new neural pathways and unexpected insights. This is how a tech engineer invents a kitchen tool or a poet rethinks a business plan.

You don't need to be an expert in everything. You just need to be curious enough to connect dots others didn't think belonged on the same page.

- **Hack 260: Cross It Over**

Take your current problem and force it through the lens of another field: "How would a gardener solve this?" "What if this were a board game rule?" Flip the framework.

- **Hack 261: Swipe from Another Shelf**

Go to a section of the bookstore (or YouTube channel) you never explore — architecture, cooking, animation, marine biology. Spend 10 minutes absorbing, then return to your challenge. You'll think differently, guaranteed.

- **Hack 262: Mash-Up Generator**

Write down five random words from different domains (e.g., "spaghetti," "space," "pirate," "magnets," "symphony"). Then brainstorm how they could all relate to your project. It's absurd. It's chaotic. And it works.

- **Hack 263: Mental Remix**

Pick two unrelated ideas or problems you're working on — then deliberately try to combine their parts. What happens when your side hustle idea collides with your parenting struggle? Or when your fitness plan meets your budgeting system? The remix can reveal shared pain points and surprising cross-solutions.

- **Hack 264: Map the Metaphor**

Take your creative challenge and turn it into a map — literally. Draw it like a journey, a dungeon crawl, a treasure hunt, or a subway map. Mapping one domain into another gives structure to chaos and helps you see blind spots and new paths.

## Think Differently, On Purpose

Creativity isn't luck. It's not lightning. It's strategy.

It's about giving your brain permission to misbehave a little — to scribble outside the lines, to try something dumb, to explore without demanding usefulness.

When you stop waiting for inspiration and start building systems that spark it, you unlock creative flow on command.

So go ahead: break the mold. Doodle the idea. Hum the problem. Scribble the weird solution. Then step back and admire the art of thinking differently.

Your brain's not broken. It's just waiting for a better playground.

# Learning on Speed

## Smarter, Faster, Retained

If you've ever read something, nodded, and then promptly forgotten 98% of it by the next day, you're not alone. That's not your memory being lazy. That's your learning method being outdated.

Most of us were taught how to *study*, but not how to *learn*. We were told to highlight, reread, and cram. But those are passive strategies—like expecting to get fit by watching someone else do push-ups.

This chapter is your shortcut to learning smarter. No 12-hour marathons or color-coded flashcards required. Just high-efficiency hacks that make knowledge stick faster and deeper—because your brain deserves better than highlighters and hope.

Let's make your learning fast, fun, and unforgettable.

### Active Recall vs Passive Review (school never taught this)

Your brain is a lazy genius. If it can avoid effort, it will. That's why rereading notes feels productive—it *feels* like you're learning, but really, you're just recognizing familiar words. Active recall, on the other hand, forces your brain to work—dragging the info out of storage and strengthening the path in the process.

Think of it like this: passive review is skimming the map; active recall is taking the route.

- **Hack 265: Close the Book Test**

After learning something, close the book and write down everything you remember. Don't cheat. The gaps you find? That's where real learning begins.

- **Hack 266: The "Explain It Ugly" Rule**

Try to explain the concept out loud like you're ranting to a friend who's half-listening. No fancy jargon—just ugly, blunt explanation. If you can do that, you get it.

- **Hack 267: Cover-and-Scribble Technique**

Cover your notes. Grab a piece of paper. Scribble what you remember. Then check what you got right. Bonus: Do it with a different-colored pen each time for tracking growth.

- **Hack 268: The Forget-and-Fetch Drill**

Step away for 30 minutes after learning something. Then come back and try to recall the 3 main ideas. No notes. Just memory. This mimics the brain's natural recall system.

## Spaced Repetition = Your Brain's BFF

Your brain doesn't learn best by brute force. It learns by intervals—like watering a plant at the right times, not flooding it all at once. Spaced repetition is the art of revisiting information just before you forget it, which strengthens memory like adding weights at the gym.

Short bursts. Spaced out. That's how smart brains build long-term storage.

- **Hack 269: The "1-2-5-10" Rule**

Review something one day after learning it, then two days later, then five, then ten. It's a memory-saving rhythm your brain will thank you for.

- **Hack 270: Flashback Fridays**

Every Friday, spend 10 minutes reviewing stuff you learned earlier in the week. No pressure. Just skim and quiz yourself. You're reinforcing without cramming.

- **Hack 271: Digital Spaced Tools**

Use apps like Anki or Mochi that automatically space your flashcards based on your recall. They do the timing; your brain does the storing.

- **Hack 272: Sticky Note Ladder**

Write key facts on sticky notes and move them across your workspace based on how well you remember them. Forget one? Move it back. Nail it? Push it forward.

## Teaching What You Learn (even if it's to a cat)

Nothing clarifies your thoughts like trying to explain them to someone else. It's why teachers always seem to know their stuff inside out. Teaching forces your brain to organize, simplify, and connect dots. Bonus points if your "student" is imaginary or furry—it still works.

- **Hack 273: Cat Classrooms**

Set a timer and "teach" the topic to your pet, houseplant, or your reflection. No notes. Just words. If you trip, that's your weak spot.

- **Hack 274: The Rubber Duck Method**

Put a small object (toy, paperweight, literal rubber duck) on your desk. Explain your current topic to it daily. You'll be shocked at how many insights pop up mid-ramble.

- **Hack 275: Write a Mini Guide**

Summarize what you've learned in under 300 words—as if you're writing a beginner's guide for a friend. Clear = stored.

- **Hack 276: Make a "One Slide Lesson"**

One slide. One image. One big idea. Teaching it visually forces simplicity and structure—two things your brain loves for recall.

## The Five-Minute Review Habit

You don't need to spend hours reviewing. Just five minutes of intentional recall can turn slippery info into sticky knowledge. Tiny review rituals keep your brain prepped and primed—like mental brushing and flossing.

It's not about quantity—it's about consistency.

- **Hack 277: Review at Transitions**

End your day, your lunch break, or a meeting with 5 minutes of recall: What did I learn? What stood out? What questions do I still have?

- **Hack 278: Shower Recaps**

While shampooing, mentally replay what you learned today. You're relaxed, unstimulated, and your brain is in great recall mode. Clean scalp, clean thoughts.

- **Hack 279: Voice Note Learning Log**

Record yourself summarizing key takeaways on your phone. Listen back while commuting or cooking. You're learning from your own voice—very meta, very effective.

- **Hack 280: The Mirror Method**

Stand in front of a mirror. Recap a lesson or idea like you're giving a TED Talk. Cringe at first, but powerful later.


## Brain-Boosting Study Snacks & Setups

You don't need a Pinterest-worthy desk or a smoothie made from moon rocks. But your learning environment and fuel *do* matter. If your space is chaos and your snacks are all trash, your brain's running with one hand tied behind its back.

Let's build a setup your brain wants to show up for.

- **Hack 281: The Protein-First Snack Rule**

Grab protein + complex carbs before a study session—think boiled eggs + whole grain toast, or nuts + fruit. It keeps your blood sugar stable and your attention wired-in.

- **Hack 282: The Learning Scent Hack**

Pick a scent (peppermint, citrus, rosemary) and use it only when studying. Your brain will associate it with focus, like Pavlov, but with brains and essential oils.

- **Hack 283: Light and Noise Tweaks**

Natural light + soft background sound = ideal brain conditions. No dungeon caves or nightclub vibes. Lo-fi beats or brown noise? Go for it.

- **Hack 284: Tidy Space = Focus Place**

Before learning, spend 60 seconds tidying your space. The clearer the environment, the less background stress. Your brain notices clutter—even if you think you don't.

## Quick Recharge: Learning Isn't Just for School

Fast learning isn't just about passing a test—it's about upgrading how you move through the world. When you know how to learn, you know how to pivot, grow, and adapt to *anything* faster.

Your brain is already brilliant. These hacks just show you how to turn the dial from "meh" to "mastery" in less time and with fewer mental knots. So next time you want to learn something new—don't stress, don't cram.

Just hack the process. The Shortcut Society way.

# Neuroplasticity Playground

## Build a Better Brain at Any Age

Ever wish your brain came with a "refresh" button? Good news: it kind of does. It's called **neuroplasticity**—the science-backed superpower that lets your brain reshape itself through experiences, challenges, and learning. Translation? You're never stuck with the brain you have now.

In this chapter, we'll explore clever ways to retrain your brain for staying sharp, flexible, and energized—without needing to solve Rubik's cubes or take cold plunges at 6 a.m. (unless you're into that). Whether you're 16 or 60, these neuro-flex tools can help you grow, adapt, and get better at... well, getting better.

The best part? You don't need hours of free time or a neuroscience degree to pull this off. Most of these hacks are sneaky-small, habit-stackable, and oddly fun. Think of this as your DIY brain renovation kit—no helmet required.

### Micro-Challenges for Macro-Gains

Your brain loves routines. They're efficient, comfy, and familiar. But those same routines can also become ruts. Neuroplasticity means your brain is capable of rewriting those defaults—whether it's how you react to stress, approach conflict, or make decisions under pressure. The first step is noticing when you're running on autopilot.

Flipping the script doesn't require dramatic reinvention. It starts with interrupting patterns. When you change the route you take, the words you use, or the assumptions you challenge, you're carving fresh grooves in your mental map. It's not just a motivational slogan—it's rewiring.

- **Hack 285: Flip Your Routine**

Use your non-dominant hand for simple tasks like brushing your teeth or stirring your coffee. It forces your brain to activate different neural circuits, which is great for mental flexibility.

- **Hack 286: Take the Backwards Walk**

Every now and then, walk backward (safely!) in an open space. This quirky movement lights up unused areas of your brain, improving balance and spatial processing.

- **Hack 287: Swap Your Seat**

Try sitting in a different spot at the dinner table or rearranging your workstation. Changing physical perspective often triggers new mental perspectives too—ideal for problem-solving ruts.

- **Hack 289: 30-Second Novelty Bursts**

Once a day, listen to a music genre you never play, try a tongue twister in a different language, or describe an object using only metaphors. These tiny jolts keep your brain alert and adaptive.

- **Hack 290: Tiny Pattern Break**

Change one thing about your daily rhythm—use your phone with your left hand, change your alarm sound, or even start brushing your teeth in a new corner. Small shifts = big neuro rewiring.

## Brain Multivitamin: Curiosity

Curiosity isn't just a personality trait—it's a neural catalyst. When you're genuinely curious, your brain releases dopamine (the motivation chemical) and forges stronger memory pathways. Basically, curiosity is a free performance enhancement.

Curiosity also shifts you into an active thinking mode. It pulls you into the moment, boosts your attention span, and even makes boring topics more digestible. And unlike willpower or motivation, curiosity doesn't burn out—it builds momentum the more you use it.

- **Hack 291: Ask the Third Why**

When you wonder something, don't stop at the first "why?" Ask "why" three times to dive deeper into the topic. It forces layered thinking and helps build mental models.

- **Hack 292: The Curiosity Jar**

Keep a jar or a note on your phone to jot down random questions or ideas that pop up. Pick one per week to explore—it keeps your brain hungry, not just busy.

- **Hack 293: Teach Me Something Random**

Once a week, ask someone to explain something they love (even if you don't think you'll care). New passions, ideas, and connections live outside your usual bubble.

- **Hack 294: Curiosity Before Clickbait**

Before Googling a random question, guess the answer first. This primes your brain to engage more deeply with the result instead of skimming and forgetting.

- **Hack 295: Re-Read the First Page**

Take a book you've read and re-read just the first page. Then try to recall how it connects to the rest. You'll spot gaps, patterns, and fresh questions—which all activate deeper brain circuits.


## The Sensory Remix

Most of us operate on autopilot with our senses—but your sensory systems are some of the best brain-building tools you've got. Mixing up your sensory input can sharpen perception, deepen memory, and improve emotional regulation.

Sensory "remixing" is like giving your brain a new interface. It wakes up sleepy circuits and encourages different regions of the brain to collaborate. Plus, it's a surprisingly calming way to feel more grounded.

- **Hack 296: Close-Eyed Coffee**

Drink your morning coffee or tea with your eyes closed. Pay attention to the warmth, aroma, and texture. This single-tasking heightens sensory awareness and strengthens mindfulness circuits.

- **Hack 297: Soundtrack Shift**

Experiment with background sounds you don't usually use, such as classical, lo-fi beats, or rainforest ambience. Different soundscapes activate unique parts of your brain.

- **Hack 298: Texture Hunt**

Challenge yourself to find and name five distinct textures in your environment—like smooth, bumpy, fuzzy, etc. It pulls your attention out of your head and into the now.

- **Hack 299: Blindfold Mapping**

Try navigating your home or a familiar space (safely!) with a blindfold for a few minutes. Your brain will recalibrate how it uses touch and sound, boosting spatial awareness.

- **Hack 300: Temperature Ping**

Hold something warm in one hand and something cold in the other. The contrast shocks your nervous system into full sensory alertness—great before a creative task.

## Mind-Bending Movements

Want a brain upgrade? Move weirdly. Unconventional movement patterns stimulate underused brain regions, improve body-brain coordination, and can even help with emotional regulation. Your brain isn't a floating head—it's wired to your body.

Physical play isn't just fun—it's transformation in disguise. These movements challenge assumptions, shake off mental cobwebs, and boost focus. It's not about being athletic. It's about being unexpected.

- **Hack 301: Cross-Crawl Reset**

March in place while tapping your opposite hand to your knee. It's silly but powerful—activates both hemispheres and resets focus when you're mentally fried.

- **Hack 302: Mirror Moves**

Do everyday gestures (like brushing your hair or picking up your bag) while watching yourself in a mirror. This boosts body awareness and strengthens visual-spatial mapping.

- **Hack 303: Animal Flow Breaks**

Take 5 minutes to try "animal" movements—bear crawls, crab walks, frog jumps. Besides waking you up, they increase neuro-muscular coordination and flexibility in thinking.

- **Hack 304: Chaotic Dance Party**

Put on a random song and dance like a malfunctioning robot. No rhythm, just randomness. Your brain has to predict, adjust, and react—exactly what neuroplasticity thrives on.

- **Hack 305: Opposite Day Workout**

If you're used to structured workouts, try free movement play. If you usually do cardio, try balancing. Unpredictability forces your brain to adapt in real-time.

## Brain Boundaries: Protect the Upgrade

Growth isn't just about adding more. It's also about saying "nope" to what dulls your thinking. Setting boundaries—around input, multitasking, or burnout—is a brain-protective move that pays long-term dividends.

Neuroplasticity needs recovery time. Your brain rewires while you rest, daydream, and digest. So protecting your attention and avoiding overload isn't laziness—it's strategic brain training.

- **Hack 306: The "One Tab Only" Rule**

When working on a mentally demanding task, keep only one browser tab open at a time. Fewer distractions = deeper thinking = better brain health.

- **Hack 307: Input Detox Hour**

Give your brain one hour daily with *zero* new input—no phone, podcasts, or music. Just quiet. Your brain uses that space to consolidate, not consume.

- **Hack 308: The 20-Second Recovery Pause**

Between mental tasks, stop for 20 seconds, close your eyes, and take three slow breaths. This tells your brain: "We're not in a panic. You can think clearly now."

- **Hack 309: Say No to "Just One More Thing"**

That impulse to squeeze in "just one more" before rest is a shortcut to burnout. Stop when you planned to stop. Give your brain a full recovery window.

- **Hack 310: Guard Your Mornings**

Don't let the first 30 minutes of your day be hijacked by email or social media. Protect that golden window for calm thinking or focused effort.

## Your Brain's Still Under Construction

Brains aren't finished products. They're playgrounds, workshops, and construction sites all rolled into one. That means there's no "too late" to start building better wiring. And no "too early," either. Whether you're 16, 60, or 96, your brain is still listening, still learning, still adapting—every single day.

Every odd little habit you try, every new connection you make, every time you choose curiosity over autopilot—you're casting a vote for the brain you want to have tomorrow. You're not stuck. You're not static. You're in motion. That's the beauty of neuroplasticity: it's not about becoming someone else. It's about becoming *more you*, but sharper, calmer, and more alive.

So break the pattern. Do the thing that feels a little awkward. Ask the weird question. Learn the strange fact. Move differently. Rest with purpose. Play like it matters—because it does. You're not here to preserve your brain. You're here to *expand* it.

Build it like a masterpiece, one surprising shortcut at a time.

# Feelings Are Data

## Emotional Intelligence for Mental Mastery

Emotions aren't obstacles to logic—they're signals. Think of them like your brain's push notifications: sometimes annoying, often messy, but usually trying to tell you something important. And just like any data stream, when you learn how to interpret those signals instead of ignoring or bulldozing them, you get smarter. Sharper. More in control.

Emotional intelligence isn't about "being soft" or suppressing feelings—it's about understanding your internal operating system well enough to make it work for you, not against you. This chapter is your shortcut to decoding your emotions, responding with more clarity, and tapping into one of the most underrated brain upgrades out there: emotional fluency.

### Pattern Spotting in Emotional Reactions

Most people think their reactions "just happen," but the truth is—they follow a pattern. Like reruns of your least-favorite sitcom, the same emotional loops can play out over and over again unless you spot the script and rewrite it. Maybe it's snapping at your partner after work, spiraling when plans change, or freezing during feedback. These aren't random—your brain's running an emotional program you forgot was even installed.

When you start identifying the pattern behind the emotion, you get out of autopilot. You become a pattern analyst for your own brain—tracking, tweaking, and eventually retraining how you respond.

- **Hack 311: Trigger Tracker**

Keep a simple log for a week—what made you frustrated, anxious, or sad? Then look for repeats. That "ugh" feeling on Mondays might not be about Mondays—it could be the 9 a.m. Zoom with that one person who interrupts you.

- **Hack 312: The 90-Second Window**

Emotions spike for about 90 seconds before your brain adds a narrative. When you feel overwhelmed, set a timer. Just breathe. Don't react. After 90 seconds, decide what's *actually* going on.

- **Hack 313: Rewind the Tape**

When you notice an outsized reaction, mentally hit rewind. Ask: "What happened 10 minutes before this?" Often, the real cause isn't the email—it's the five micro-stressors that came before it.

## Building Your Emotional Vocabulary

You can't fix what you can't name—and most people are stuck using "stressed," "fine," or "annoyed" to describe a galaxy of emotional states. But the words you use shape your brain's interpretation of reality. A richer emotional vocabulary doesn't just make you better at talking about your feelings—it actually helps your brain regulate them more effectively.

Think of it like upgrading from dial-up to fiber. More bandwidth means more clarity, less misfire, and faster emotional processing.

- **Hack 314: Upgrade from 'Fine'**

Ban the word "fine" from your self-check-ins for a day. Instead, choose from a list of emotions—disappointed, tense, hopeful, embarrassed, etc. Challenge yourself to be specific.

- **Hack 315: Emoji Check-Ins**

Not feeling wordy? Use emojis to reflect how you're feeling. This visual method can help identify complex feelings when words are hard to access.

- **Hack 316: Feeling Wheel Flip**

Google "Feeling Wheel" and pick one emotion. Then flip it: what's the opposite? This expands your emotional range and builds balance in how you process both positive and negative states.

## Using Emotions for Smarter Decisions

We like to think we're logical creatures who sometimes feel—but it's the other way around. Emotions influence nearly every decision we make, whether we admit it or not. The shortcut isn't to eliminate emotion from your choices (that's not possible)—it's to understand *why* you feel what you feel so you can make better decisions with that data.

When you decode the emotional "why," your decisions gain depth, speed, and staying power. This isn't about cold, robotic logic—it's about choosing with your whole brain.

- **Hack 317: Gut Scan**

Before making a decision, ask: "What emotion am I feeling about this?" Then ask: "What's that emotion trying to protect or promote?" Often, that's the hidden priority your rational mind missed.

- **Hack 318: Logic + Emotion Grid**

Draw a 2x2 grid with high/low emotion and high/low logic. Where does your decision land? Aim for high logic + acknowledged emotion = smart + human decision-making.

- **Hack 319: Future You Filter**

Ask: "What would Future Me thank me for?" Emotions usually care about *now*—this flips your focus to what matters most in the long run.

## Fast Emotional Resets for Mental Clarity

We like to think we're logical creatures who sometimes feel—but it's the other way around. Emotions influence nearly every decision we make, whether we admit it or not. The shortcut isn't to eliminate emotion from your choices (that's not possible)—it's to understand *why* you feel what you feel so you can make better decisions with that data.

When you decode the emotional "why," your decisions gain depth, speed, and staying power. This isn't about cold, robotic logic—it's about choosing with your whole brain.

- **Hack 320: Ice Trick Reset**

Hold an ice cube in your hand for 30 seconds when spiraling. It shocks your nervous system into the present moment, grounding you quickly.

- **Hack 321: Change the Room, Change the Mood**

Leave the space you're in. Step outside, move to a different room, or change lighting. Physical change breaks emotional inertia.

- **Hack 322: 'Name + Move' Method**

Say the emotion out loud: "This is anxiety." Then move your body—shake out your arms, walk in a circle, jump once. Naming + motion disrupts emotional looping.

## Micro-Expressions & Social Cues (Decode Like Sherlock)

Not every emotional spiral needs a therapy session or a deep dive. Sometimes, you just need a mental defibrillator—a quick reset to stop the spiral before it eats the rest of your day. Emotional regulation isn't about denying feelings. It's about disrupting the loop long enough to make a conscious choice.

These fast resets give your brain a micro-break and your body a chance to exit fight-or-flight. Think of them as brain CPR.

- **Hack 323: The 3-Second Face Freeze**

When talking to someone, glance at their face the moment a topic shifts. That fleeting expression before the "social mask" reappears? That's the truth.

- **Hack 324: Feet Don't Lie**

Pay attention to someone's feet in a conversation. Are they pointed toward you or the door? Subtle but telling—people often reveal intent with posture before words.

- **Hack 325: Mirroring Scan**

Are they mirroring your body language? If yes, they're probably engaged. If not, you may be losing them—or they're not comfortable. Adjust your tone or approach accordingly.

## You Can Think With Your Heart (Strategically)

Emotions aren't enemies of logic—they're part of your cognitive toolkit. When you treat them as data instead of distractions, your brain doesn't just get smarter—it gets wiser. The trick is learning to listen without being led, to feel without being flooded, and to decide with both head and heart.

So go ahead. Feel your feels. Track the patterns. Decode the faces. And remember: the emotionally intelligent brain? That's the one who leads the room *and* keeps its cool.

# You Don't Need a New Brain

## Just a Few New Tricks

So here we are—at the end of a book about beginnings.

Not the kind of flashy beginnings that start with a gym membership or a 5 a.m. cold plunge. We're talking about subtle, sustainable, internal rewiring. The kind of fresh starts that come from learning how your brain actually works, then using that knowledge to nudge it forward. One curiosity, one hack, one shortcut at a time.

The truth? You've always had a hackable brain. This book just held up the blueprint.

### The Real Superpower Is Self-Awareness

By now, you've probably noticed a theme running through every chapter: your brain is adaptable. Not because it's perfect, but because it's responsive. Responsive to curiosity, to effort, to small changes, and even to boredom. Every weird experiment, focused moment, and reframed thought builds your mental muscles.

Even reading this far proves something powerful: you're not passively drifting through life. You're someone who wants to think sharper, feel clearer, and act more intentionally. That's not a small thing. That's the foundation of everything.

Self-awareness is what gives every hack in this book its power. The moment you pause and ask, "What's really going on in my head right now?" is the moment you start taking control. And that's a skill no one can take away from you.

Forget needing to become a productivity ninja or a memory champion. You've already done something 99% of people won't—you've slowed down long enough to learn how your brain works. And now? You know where the light switches are.

**Celebrate Progress, Not Perfection**

Let's say it louder for the perfectionists in the back: **you don't need to do everything in this book**.

If you just try *one* hack from each chapter, you're rewiring your routines. If you go all in on a few favorites, you'll see real-world results—more clarity, less brain fog, better recall, and stronger decision-making. And if you fall off the wagon for a few days (or weeks)? No shame. Shortcut Society rule #1: **progress over perfection**.

We're not here to build the "perfect" brain. We're here to build a flexible one. A playful one. One that recovers faster, learns deeper, and keeps evolving.

Brains aren't machines. They're ecosystems. And just like any good garden, they respond best to care, variety, and a little mess now and then.

**Make the Book Work for You (Not the Other Way Around)**

This isn't a one-and-done read. It's a tool chest.

Flip back to the hacks that resonated. Mark them. Star them. Share them. Use sticky notes. Scribble in the margins. Make it yours.

Better yet—use it when things *don't* feel sharp. When your motivation tanks, when your memory ghosts you, or when stress builds like a pressure cooker—open the book at random. See what pops out. You'll be surprised how often the exact right shortcut finds you when you need it.

The real win isn't in remembering all the tricks. It's in knowing they're there when you need them. This book is your mental Swiss Army knife. Pull it out anytime you feel stuck.

And remember: most of these hacks don't require spare hours or perfect conditions. You don't need silence, structure, or a standing desk. You just need five minutes and a brain. Lucky you.

**Keep Experimenting. Keep Adjusting. Keep Playing.**

Shortcut Society readers don't wait for life to be ideal. They make small moves that spark momentum.

The only difference between someone who says, "I wish I were better at X" and someone who *is* better? Experiments. Curiosity. Trial and error.

The good news is, your brain *wants* to help you. It wants patterns, progress, and purpose. Give it those things in small doses, and it will build new highways for your thoughts to travel.

If something doesn't work for you? That's not failure. That's feedback. Try a different hack. Stack two small ones together. Adjust the dosage. Make it playful. Make it yours.

You're never "done" building your brain. Which is a great thing, because it means you're never stuck. Whether you're recovering from burnout or chasing your next level, the same tools apply: movement, reflection, reframing, boundaries, breath, novelty, focus, and rest.

It's not about doing more. It's about doing what *works*—for *you*.

**The Shortcut Mindset: What Changes Everything**

There's a reason we called this series the Shortcut Society. Not because we believe in skipping the work, but because we believe in removing the friction.

A shortcut is a smarter route. It gets you to the same (or better) destination with less stress, fewer detours, and more energy left over. That's not cheating. That's evolving.

You don't need to hustle harder. You don't need to shame yourself into focus. You need to step back, zoom out, and ask: "What would make this easier? Faster? More fun?"

Brains are built to optimize. And now, so are you.

So whether you're planning your week, navigating conflict, brainstorming a new project, or trying to remember where you left your phone for the fourth time—pause. Breathe. Hack it.

### And If You Forget Everything Else...

Here are a few truths worth underlining:

- **Mental fog doesn't mean you're broken.** It means you need space, sleep, or a new input.
- **You don't need to hustle harder.** You need to hack smarter.
- **Growth isn't loud or flashy.** It's the quiet decision to try again when no one's watching.
- **Your brain isn't a black box.** It's a living, learning, adapting machine. And you're the operator.

So whenever you're tempted to power through, check out, or spiral into the "I'll never figure this out" loop—pause. Flip back. Pick a hack. Try something.

That's how real change happens.


### Welcome to Your Upgraded Brain

You don't need a degree in neuroscience. You don't need to meditate in a cave. And you certainly don't need a brand new brain. You just need a few new tricks—and the permission to use them.

Now you have both.

Keep hacking. Keep adjusting. Keep asking better questions. Your brain will thank you.

And if anyone ever asks how you got so sharp, focused, or resilient?

Just smile and say: *"Shortcut Society."*

www.ingramcontent.com/pod-product-compliance
Lightning Source LLC
Chambersburg PA
CBHW052111070526
44584CB00017B/2432